Contents

Acknowledgments

The authors would like to thank Rosalind Rosenberg, Kathy Neckerman, and Howie Winant for reading earlier drafts of chapters 2, 3, and 4, respectively.

Bev also thanks Alice Kessler-Harris, Rafael Lantigua, and Thomas Neal, Karin, Muriel and, of course, Alexander for their nurture and support. Lynn, as always, thanks Patricia Clough, Wendy Simonds and, of course, Michael and her Alexander for their ongoing love and inspiration. We would also like to thank Ken Provencher, Kelvin Matthews, and Valevy Rose for their help in bringing this project to fruition.

Most of all, though, the authors would like to express gratitude to all their students of "Gender, Race, and Class" at Barnard College/Columbia University and Fordham University. Without their insights, this book would not have been possible.

Gender, Race, and Class

3/97

UNIVERSITY OF WOLVERHAMPTON
ENTERPRISE LTD.

LR/LEND/002

Harrison Learning Centre
Wolverhampton Campus
University of Wolverhampton
St Peter's Square
Wolverhampton WV1 1RH
Telephone: 0845 408 1631

ONE WEEK LOAN

1 - MAR 2007		
1 3 MAR 2008	2 4 DEC 2012	
3 0 NOV 2009		

Telephone Renewals: 01902 321333
Please RETURN this item on or before the last date shown above.
Fines will be charged if items are returned late.
See tariff of fines displayed at the Counter. (L2)

21st-Century Sociology

SERIES EDITOR: Steven Seidman, State University of New York at Albany

The *21st-Century Sociology* series provides instructors and students with key texts in sociology that speak with a distinct sociological voice and offer thoughtful and original perspectives. The texts reflect current discussions in and beyond sociology, avoiding standard textbook definitions to engage students in critical thinking and new ideas. Prominent scholars in various fields of social inquiry combine theoretical perspectives with the latest research to present accessible syntheses for students as we move further into the new millennium amidst rapid social change.

Gender, Race, and Class

An Overview

LYNN S. CHANCER AND
BEVERLY XAVIERA WATKINS

Blackwell
Publishing

© 2006 by Lynn S. Chancer and Beverly Xaviera Watkins

BLACKWELL PUBLISHING
350 Main Street, Malden, MA 02148-5020, USA
9600 Garsington Road, Oxford OX4 2DQ, UK
550 Swanston Street, Carlton, Victoria 3053, Australia

First published 2006 by Blackwell Publishing Ltd

1 2006

Library of Congress Cataloging-in-Publication Data

Chancer, Lynn S., 1954–
Gender, race, and class : an overview / Lynn
S. Chancer and Beverly Xaviera Watkins.
  p. cm. – (21st-century sociology)
  Includes bibliographical references and index.
ISBN-13: 978-0-631-22034-3 (hardback : alk. paper)
ISBN-10: 0-631-22034-8 (hardback : alk. paper)
ISBN-13: 978-0-631-22035-0 (pbk. : alk. paper)
ISBN-10: 0-631-22035-6 (pbk. : alk. paper)
  1. Equality–United States. 2. United States–Race relations.
3. Sex role–United States. 4. Social classes–United States.
5. Prejudices –United States. 6. Discrimination–United States.
I. Watkins, Beverly Xaviera II. Title. III. Series.

  HN90.S6C485 2006
  305′.0973–dc22

                                          2005017739

A catalogue record for this title is available from the British Library.

Set in 10/12.5pt Photina
by SPI Publisher Services, Pondicherry, India
Printed and bound in United Kingdom
by TJ International, Padstow, Cornwal

For further information on
Blackwell Publishing, visit our website:
www.blackwellpublishing.com

CHAPTER ONE

Introduction: Why Gender, Race, and Class?

Between 1991 and 1998, the seven years I taught full-time in the Sociology Departments of Barnard College and Columbia University, I was best known for my cross-listed course entitled "Gender, Race, and Class." At the time, the topic was surely at the pinnacle of its popularity not only at Barnard/Columbia but at campuses across the country. A textbook on this subject by sociologist Patricia Hill Collins had quickly become a huge bestseller; intersectionality was being used widely as a term across a range of disciplines.[1] New departments and programs had sprung up in African American Studies, Gender (not only Women's) Studies, Latino Studies, and other areas. These confirmed how much values of difference and pluralism – and the downplaying of false universalisms – had gained students' and professors' attentions. Given this context, it was hardly surprising that my course offering regularly attracted great interest, drawing between 150 and 200 undergraduates and sometimes graduate students from a panoply of fields in the social sciences as well as from across the humanities.

During these same years, though, I was also teased on a fairly regular basis by other sociologists about this well-known – at least on the Barnard/Columbia campuses – association with "Gender, Race, and Class." While some students thought the subject matter "cool," some of my more conventional sociological colleagues mused that my popularity as a professor derived mostly from my teaching a currently faddish topic; in this respect, the association had what Erving Goffman called a negative contagion effect. One friend, a male sociologist also cynically inclined on this matter, asked why call the course "Gender, Race, and Class"? Why not call it "Gender, Race, Class, Age, Sexuality, Queer Theory, and Nationality"? he would only half-jokingly inquire. To him, the three terms sounded like a mantra that had become enmeshed in obligatory fashion demanded by political correctness. What such cynics shared, each in his/her own way, was doubt that gender, race, and class – however well subscribed – was a serious and rigorous subject of study.

Consequently by the late 1990s, in keeping with other trends that led Susan Faludi to express concerns about anti-feminist reactions and Stephen Steinberg to worry that gains in racial equality were being turned back, I found that teaching this course had placed me in a paradoxical position. On the one hand, some people were calling courses on gender, race, and class the flavor of the moment, a taste not necessarily seen as justifiable through its intellectual contents alone. On the other hand, in the many years that I have now been a professor, I am sure that "Gender, Race, and Class" has been the best – by which I mean the most intellectually satisfying – course from students' perspectives of any that I have taught. I became convinced of this partly on the basis of the sheer number of students who contact me years later about how deeply the course had affected their long-term careers and now-honed critical faculties. But, inside myself, I also have a sense of satisfaction from knowing both that the course has been well structured and that it has sparked what C. Wright Mills wonderfully dubbed my own and others' "sociological imaginations."[2]

It was precisely because of this odd defensiveness about a course I believed (and have been reinforced in believing) to be excellent that I agreed to write this book. My co-author is Beverly Watkins who, over the years of her exposure as a teaching assistant to material and students in "Gender, Race, and Class," also became my friend. Both of us know that, of course, courses on gender, race, and class – like any other academic department and area – emerged alongside interrelated historical and political developments. Yet we also understand that some topics deserve more than others, by dint of the sheer academic richness they impart, to be taught and re-taught. Thus our perspective in this volume is a stubborn one: for reasons as much intellectual as politic, we think that indeed gender, race, and class is an area of study likely to resonate in social science for decades to come. Our purpose here is to show, both theoretically and concretely, why.

One reason for this assertion is easy and clear-cut. Ironically gender, race, and class refer to what are already acknowledged to be standard, classic dimensions of the social world. These terms are basic ingredients of most social scientists' repertoires, so much so as to make departments without courses on these subjects virtually impossible to imagine. Still, traditionally, sociology departments have been likely to feature courses on the sociology of sex and gender, the sociology of race/ethnicity, the sociology of class, but not necessarily strong ones on how these dimensions of the social world interrelate. No doubt, connections among these dimensions are routinely emphasized in separate courses on gender, race/ethnicity, and class but their analytic interconnections are not these courses' *raison d'être*. On the contrary, at its best, teaching a course on gender, race, and class demands exploration by professors and students of exactly how these aspects of sociology need to be co-considered lest the complexity of our day-to-day social world is underestimated or overlooked.

A second reason to insist that courses on gender, race, and class are significant on purely intellectual grounds is a bit subtler. For teaching "Gender, Race, and Class" – that is, highlighting connections between several dimensions of the social world rather than focusing on just one – can call attention to questions of commonalities as well as differences. Certainly, it is the latter that was emphasized through the 1990s more than the former during the so-called "culture wars" that pitted feminists, gay and racial equality activists, and progressive leftists against forces of backlash. As this volume will underscore, writings about difference – between women and men, races and ethnicities and classes, straights and gays – have had very valid points, mocking simplistic claims of a universal humanity with neatly aligned motivations, interests, and goals. Yet probing deeper also suggests that underlying distinctive forms of gender, race, and class discrimination may also – and this is meant as a both/and rather than an either/or statement about commonalities and differences – be similar sentiments that arise when human beings show disdain for the characteristics, be they gendered, racialized, or class-based, of others. Consequently, as we shall see in both this book's introduction and ensuing chapters, perhaps gender, class, and race differences cannot be satisfyingly discussed unless the question of why discriminatory biases so stubbornly persist is also seriously probed.

How, then, is this volume organized to explore both these themes – the first related to connections between gender, race, and class and the second to the simultaneous importance of exploring commonalities and differences? Based on the course I have now taught for years on both undergraduate and graduate levels at Barnard/Columbia and Fordham University, this book is structured around five chapters. In the rest of this introductory chapter 1, we elaborate a conceptual vocabulary that will be used throughout this text for the dual goals just mentioned. Here, we present five ideas that have proved to be extremely useful, and which arise again and again, in the study of gender, race, and class in the United States and abroad. Then, in chapters 2, 3, and 4, we continue with chapters that are themselves aimed at fulfilling two objectives. The first half of each of these chapters introduces the study of gender, race, and class respectively by providing what we hope are practical overviews of extant theories. How can gender be defined and understood? What are various ways of defining and discussing race? Finally, what are the main intellectual frameworks that have been used in the study of class? As students have told me over the years, these overviews may or may not be something available to them in other courses; moreover, being presented with clear definitions of each subject matter in the same course, and now in the same volume, allows immediate comparisons to be made.

But the second half of each chapter goes farther. In the chapter on gender, after reviewing three ways of defining this area of study, we proceed with the question "What has been left out of this picture?" Here our objective is to exemplify, as clearly as possible, problems bequeathed and benefits created when taking race into account as a way of rendering our understanding of gender more complex and multi-dimensional. Similarly, in chapter 3's discussion of race, we turn to complexities that arise when introducing issues of gender and class into the study of race as a social/sociological category. Last but not at all least, after chapter 4's discussion of various paradigms of class, we will look at the consequences of ignoring (and the greater richness resultant from introducing) considerations of race and gender.

Chapter 5, aimed at bringing together the material previously discussed, looks at ongoing debates within each area. For instance, we discuss feminist debates over sex and sexuality that have dealt with race and class secondarily. This concluding chapter attempts to show where serious analytic omissions can arise from approaches that prioritize gender, race, or class rather than treating their separate contributions more synthetically. This chapter also examines well-known studies – for instance, Philippe Bourgois's ethnography of drug dealing in East Harlem entitled *In Search of Respect* – that have consciously sought to incorporate gender, race, and class perspectives. Before proceeding, it should also be noted that most (if not all) of the examples used in this text are US-based, these being the instances and the literature with which we were most familiar. However, our hope is that the analytical perspectives and tools presented here can be usefully applied to a variety of other national and/or international contexts, even if we have not been able to do so fully ourselves. What are the intellectual advantages of a more multi-dimensional sociological sensibility, and have attempts at such incorporation worked? Chapter 5 also broaches, by way of conclusion, questions of social theory to which this book intends to contribute. These questions include the extent to which this subject matter may have the potential for shedding light on deeper questions of why and how human beings come to discriminate, with often terrible consequences, in the first place.

With this organizational map in hand, then, let us begin by establishing a common conceptual vocabulary on which readers can rely in pages and chapters to come.

Useful Concepts for Studying Gender, Race, and Class

Each time I have taught "Gender, Race, and Class," I have begun by presenting a set of concepts to be used, and re-used, across a wide range of examples, some drawn from popular culture and news events and others more conventionally from sociological and other academic literatures. By now, five concepts need preliminary explanation since they reappear throughout substantive chapters to come:

1. Determinism/essentialism versus social constructionism
2. Universalism versus cultural relativism/historical specificity
3. Reductionism/autonomy versus complexity
4. Chancer's A/B/C analytic framework
5. Identity versus coalition politics

Note that most of these concepts take the form of antinomies, posing one idea against another as the terms have often been opposed in actually unfolding debates. In some situations, both aspects of these debates may have validity and synthetic approaches seem desirable; in other cases, as also sometimes happens, synthetic approaches are difficult or logically impossible to manage. Soon to be seen, though, is that "Chancer's A/B/C framework," as we have caled it, is a tool of analysis rather than an opposition per se.

I   Determinism/essentialism versus social constructionism

This is one of the oldest ongoing debates in social science, one that counterposes beliefs in unchanging ongoing essences of phenomena to an equally passionate conviction that social life, as we know it, results from interactive processes over which human beings exert control. To say that something is determined is to assert that it has been made this way by a law of nature, by biology, and that little can be done to alter what appears. In regard to building a common conceptual vocabulary for studying gender, race, and class, determinism can also be used fairly interchangeably with the term essentialism. In philosophy, essentialism has been opposed by phenomenologists to existence; the former refers to that which is unchanging in things, and the latter to the dynamic and constantly changing facets of life and human consciousness.

On the other hand, the history of social construction in the social sciences has been one of rebelling against the apparent intransigence of essentialism as well as determinism. Constructionists focus on what has been created by, for, and among human beings, and have been understandably concerned about confusing what people have themselves/ourselves created (by our practices, actions, thought processes, body language) with what supposedly just is as a result of nature. Thus, in works such as Peter Berger and Thomas Luckmann's *The Social Construction of Reality* and John Berger's *Ways of Seeing*, these authors beautifully demonstrate how human actions and perceptions have molded, and therefore have the potential to un-mold as well, the social world we otherwise might take as given and unchangeable.[3]

But how, more precisely, does this apply to our topic at hand? Regarding gender: Freud's famous dictum, "Biology is destiny," was a deterministic and essentialistic statement. While at other moments subtler in his thinking, Freud in this phrase asserted that women's character has been genetically fixed; their/our essential traits have been biologically programmed by nature rather than by culture or nurture. Thus, if women appear to be passive, this is because they/we were born this way, essentially and deterministically. Evidently, though, a social constructionist would make exactly the opposite interpretation. To the extent a nineteenth-century woman in Freud's time may have seemed passive, a social constructionist – whether John Stuart Mill or twentieth-century radical feminists – would hold that women had few opportunities to become otherwise. Their apparent passivity had been constructed as the result of a male-dominated society; nothing about it was given, determined, essential, and certainly not immutable.

Examples in the area of race are equally obvious. The history of sociobiology has been punctuated regularly with attempts to justify racial inferiority on deterministic or essential, and ultimately on biologically based, grounds. For instance, to assert that American blacks are racially inferior because less intelligent than American whites is obviously to make a deterministic and essentialistic statement; it is to assert, on seemingly biological grounds alone, that one race is less intelligent than another. On the other hand, social constructionists would hasten to say – in contemporary context – that any evidence of lower SAT scores, for instance, on the part of minorities results from a host of disadvantages that themselves emanate from a long and virulent history of discrimination. Rather than SAT scores being correlated with intelligence, a constructionist would contend, these result primarily from social status and class; children in well-to-do areas are tutored to learn how to test-take whereas the poor have disproportionately received secondary educations. According to the social constructionist, then, this outcome has virtually nothing to do with biology, and basically everything to do with how we have arranged society.

Sociobiological debates over intelligence – and therefore debates about determinism/essentialism versus social constructionism – continue to surface in era after era. As applied to racism, controversy was vigorously stirred by the 1996 publication of an 800-page tome: *The Bell Curve* recycled precisely this debate.[4] Written by Richard Herrnstein (known for his sociobiological leanings) and Charles Murray, *The Bell Curve* contended that inequality in American society resulted from IQ differentials that were themselves tied to biological predispositions. Yet, as five senior Berkeley professors counter-contended in a volume called *Inequality by Design* (expressly written in response to *The Bell Curve*), Herrnstein and Murray's account could not explain why some ethnic groups who fall at the bottom of some societies then rise to the top when they immigrate to other societies. According to Claude Fischer et al., the rapidity of such changes contradicts essentialistic notions, underscoring by contrast the huge influence of socially constructed arrangements. In other words, it is designed inequality that explains social groups' accomplishments or lack thereof much more than anything determined or intrinsic in biological terms.[5]

2   Universalism versus cultural relativism/historical specificity

"Universalism" in this context takes us back to Enlightenment notions of rights and equality, and also to humanistic philosophies from which these ideas have historically emanated. More specifically, by this usage, a universalistic view is one that prioritizes how a given social experience or practice – let's say, for illustration's sake, death – recurs across any, and perhaps all, social contexts we can imagine. Thus the experience of death seems indeed to be universal: do we know of any society, at any time, which has managed to avoid this for even one of its members indefinitely? Analogously, one could say that human beings universally require to be fed and to drink lest we die; humanists might go further yet to contend that all human beings are born with rights whether or not properly granted and realized.

On the other hand, commentators who have stressed cultural relativism and historical specificity – often to correct for what they see as irresponsibly blithe assertions of commonality on the part of universalists – emphasize variations in human experiences and practices in different places and at different times. Thus, a cultural relativist may be less interested in death's obvious universality than in how – in relation to a given nation, sect, ethnic, or racial group and, no doubt, relative to religion – perceptions and reactions to our mortality decidedly differ. A party whose concern is historical specificity may also, or instead, be interested in whether attitudes on death have stayed the same over decades or centuries. For this observer, attitudes toward death may relax and evolve with time so that any claims to the universality of death must be evaluated specifically in regard to historical contexts of perception/reception.

This discussion can be more or less argumentative but is virtually bound to arise, literally and figuratively, in the study of gender, race, and class. For instance, as the next chapter on gender explains, the unfolding of various feminisms was partially spurred by disagreements over whether a basic radical feminist concept – the notion of patriarchy, or male domination as a basic structural characteristic of societies – existed in all places and times. Detractors felt that radical feminist theorists had used the idea as though universally applicable to all societies. But, bracketing the question of whether or not these critics' point is valid, counter-claims illustrate debates over universalism as opposed to cultural relativism and historical specificity. For the relativist, claims to patriarchy's universality overlook that practices appearing to manifest male domination may, in some societies, be perceived quite differently – for example, as reflecting a mutually agreed-upon gendered division of labor. More concretely yet, this universalist versus cultural relativism debate has been applied to analyses of clitorectomies. For some relativists, Western critiques of what seems on its face to be a brutal practice – one that causes pain and the cessation of pleasure (pleasure and pain being arguably universalistic concepts) – fail to grasp that women in non-Western societies may not perceive these operations as oppressive but, instead, as an accepted (maybe even acceptable) part and parcel of cultures to which they belong. Again, how a given reader responds to this debate, whether in sync with the universalist and horrified at the culturalist (or vice versa), matters less for the moment than exemplifying the persistence of such debates in this sociological subfield.

Take, as one further example, debates over race. A universalist might wish to claim that race is a universal concept; he or she might dare a listener to name one society in which some notion of racialization has not existed. On the other hand, the cultural relativist (who here may also sound very much like a social constructionist) is likely to stress huge variations in how "race" is perceived or, for that matter, whether it is used as a social classification at all. Thus, as many scholars have noted, Brazil offers a fascinating comparison with the United States in matters of racial classifications. Whereas the USA has until recently discussed race over-simplistically (in dichotomized terms of black and white or, on the census, in terms of black, white, and Hispanic), Brazilian society lists more than 200 forms of racial classification in its own social record-keeping. Consequently, concepts of racialization must be viewed as relative to particular societies rather than as reflective of underlying and supposedly universal realities. Some social theorists take debates over race even further, arguing that domination ensues from the very fact of racialization itself; for these theorists, just as racial classifications have been constructed in certain times and in particular ways, so a desirable social goal can be to undo them, thereby allowing their alleged relevance to wither away.

3   Reductionism/autonomy versus complexity

Just as the first two debates recur in courses on gender, race and class, so does – and will – the following conceptual distinction arise over and over again in illustrations and discussions to come. Reductionism can be defined as attributing the causes of a particular social phenomenon to a single factor rather than to a complex of causes; as a social analyst, a reductionist therefore tends to treat that factor as autonomous rather than interactive. To this, on the other hand, one can counterpose a commitment to complexity – to "complexifying," a term I have coined only half-jokingly and iconoclastically when teaching – wherein a commentator regularly investigates a host of possibly relevant influences to explain a phenomenon at hand.

Because these concepts' importance will be shown in many later instances, let me limit myself here to just a few examples by way of introduction. The next chapter on gender discusses critiques made by Marxist feminists of radical feminists such as Shulamith Firestone and Kate Millett about omitting sufficient attention to class. Another way of stating this

critique is that some Marxist feminists believe that radical feminists reduced the study of women's subordination to a function of gender – or
male domination – alone. In so doing capitalism's contribution to that
subordination, and the relevance in general of class differentials to understanding women's situation, was overlooked. Ironically though, this ac-
cusation of reductionism (or attributing the cause of one type of
discrimination primarily to one factor) was also exactly the objection
that Shulamith Firestone lodged against previous Marxist perspectives in
her well-known radical feminist work *The Dialectic of Sex.* According to
Firestone, Marxists, as exemplified in Engels' writings on the family,
traditionally assumed that women's subordination was entirely a product
of the capitalist system.[6] In other words, patriarchal domination of
women by men would rise and fall with capitalism's own fate; if class
inequality faded away, so presumably too would gender inequalities. This
amounted, then, to a different application of a reductionist critique. In
Firestone's opinion, many Marxists reduced gender oppression to a function of class, attributing primary explanatory power for gender biases to
class-based inequalities rather than to a more complicated combination of
social factors.

Just as this gender example will be explained in more detail in the
chapter to come, so a second example – the race/class debate that still
emerges in academic and policy contexts – will be developed later on in
further depth. Suffice it for now to say that parties on both sides of this
debate tend to accuse those on the other of reductionism of trying to
explain whether race or class inequities better accounts for ongoing
discriminations encountered in the lives of many American minorities.
Thus, sociologist Stephen Steinberg has criticized William Julius Wilson
for attributing so much importance to class in explaining obstacles
encountered by African Americans that he overlooks the ongoing relevance of racial biases. In the terminology we are using here, then, Steinberg was in effect accusing Wilson of reducing racial discrimination to a
function of class. On the other hand, the entirety of Wilson's writings –
from his first well-known work *The Declining Significance of Race* through
The Truly Disadvantaged, and *When Work Disappears* – has focused on the
enormous relevance of class.[7] To Wilson class inequities, not racial ones,
were the single most significant determinant of African Americans' life
chances. It should be noted that, in fairness, both Steinberg and Wilson
are well aware that both race and class matter. Yet, either could criticize
the other for reductionism in the sense of attributing primary explanatory
power to one social variable more than others.

4 Chancer's A/B/C Analytic Framework

While reductionism as opposed to complexity will reappear in example after example within chapters to come, so too will an analytic schema that frequently becomes relevant to understanding gender, race, and class. Central to the study of gender, race, and class are also questions of stratification, that is, exploring the way in which these and other social dimensions occur in overlapping layers relative to one another. For soon to be seen is that parties (both individuals and social groups or subgroups) who frequently experience power in one dimension of their lives may feel powerless in another. Indeed, one can hypothesize that power in one social arena may actually compensate for powerlessness encountered in another, allowing greater insight into how – if not yet why – social strata are maintained and reproduced. Such stratification can be visualized through what could be called an "A/B/C" diagram into which varied examples can be respectively fit.

By way of exemplification, imagine that a working-class white man is situated in the B position in this diagram. Sociologically speaking, this particular man may work at a job where he regularly experiences a sense of powerlessness in relation to a middle- or upper-class man who is his manager. Perhaps, for example, he is a messenger who reports to several male partners at a law firm who are clearly, in class as well as day-to-day operational terms, his superior. We could therefore place one of the upper-class male partners at his law firm in an A position. However while this working class man is relatively powerless at his workplace, he experiences far more relative power at the end of the day in a traditionally organized home as head of the household. There, in gendered terms relative to his wife, he is more powerful than powerless. Consequently, in our A/B/C diagram, his wife would occupy the C position; indeed, the powerlessness her husband often experiences at his job may feel a little easier to bear because of the greater power he feels upon coming home.

What is useful about this schema is not only that it can be applied to a host of vastly different examples but that it also suggests an extended regress of social relations beyond such A/B/C triads alone. For perhaps the male associate to whom the male messenger reports is himself subordinate to a higher male (or for that matter female) head of the law firm: now the diagram needs to be extended, conceptually at least, beyond itself at its top. Analogously, a wife who may feel relatively powerless when facing her husband may know she is also very much the boss relative to her children; again, the diagram needs to be extended beyond itself at its bottom. Common to each and all of these examples is that they provide insight into how complex gender, race and class relationships may stay in place and become reproduced.

5   Identity versus coalition politics

This last concept brings a more explicitly political dimension into the common conceptual vocabulary presented here since studying gender, race, and class points toward social movements that have played an enormous role in bringing these forms of social relationships – apart and together – to public notice. Indeed, as hinted earlier, the emergence of courses on gender, race, and class in the 1980s as opposed to the 1950s is impossible to understand unless placed in a post-1960s social movement context. Without the flowering of the feminist movement, movements for racial equality, and ongoing left politics through the 1960s, courses of this kind – and this text itself – would not have been born.

But arguably most crucial to this course's emergence were movements of identity politics. This term refers to social movements that saw as their prime purpose advocacy for individuals and groups directly affected by forms of social discrimination. Often these forms of discrimination are based on the physical characteristics or sexual practices of such individuals or groups. Thus, the feminist and civil rights movement fought against prejudice toward women and racial minorites respectively; the gay and lesbian rights movement defined itself around advocating for sexual freedom and against homophobic biases. Going back to the context of the 1960s and 1970s, identity figured into these movements' self-definitions in two ways. First, as could analogously be said for the other movements, most early feminists presumed that the concept of "woman" was a major defining identity – taking precedence above all other ways of defining oneself – for individuals associated with this cause. Similarly, being black was a critical source of identity for African Americans involved with the civil rights movement and being gay for activists involved with gay liberation. Secondly, and relatedly, identity politics therefore presumes that the people most likely to push for social recognition are individuals whose "identities" depend on these movements' successes. Thus, according to identity politics' perspectives, men are less likely to initiate actions on behalf of women; whites are less likely to start racial justice organizations; straights are less likely than those who are lesbian and gay to fight militantly against homophobia.

On the other hand, studying gender, race, and class in 2005 allows identity movements to be placed on an even broader contextual landscape. As postmodern and poststructuralist perspectives became influential through the 1980s and 1990s, work started to be written referring to terms like "fractured identities" and on "the decentered self." No longer was it clear, or believed by many scholars and activists, that one identity was foremost; rather, a given party lives out numerous capacities and dimensions that interact in extremely complex ways. Thus, a given person who is gendered also obviously has been affected by dimensions of race, ethnicity, class, age, nationality, as well as by his or her day-to-day experiences as parent, cousin, friend, and so on. This makes political affiliation on the basis of only one identity simplistic or impossible.

For some people, this has led to the replacement of identity politics by a wider coalition politics wherein a wide range of people may march in public arenas to support various causes. In the realm of social theory, this perspective has also led to queer theory which questions any notion of essence of sexual identity that appears to be fixed. Thus, already, our common conceptual vocabulary can start to be applied insofar as practitioners of coalition politics (and theorists influenced by poststructuralism) may well criticize identity politics as being essentialistic or deterministic. For such critics, the categories "woman," "Latino," or "gay" can appear fixed and unchanging, thereby partaking of the very rigidity which sustained discriminatory systems in the first place. Indeed, this is precisely the perspective Judith Butler proposed in her poststructuralist work of feminism – now arguably a contemporary feminist classic – *Gender Trouble*.[8] For Butler, there is no essence of woman or gay for that matter. Consequently, in her view, social movements are more potentially liberatory to the extent they do not reinforce or reify the very social categories which led to their creation.

With these five ideas, one can say that both a common conceptual vocabulary has been laid out and some basic tools have been provided through which relationships between gender, race, and class – and political relations that arise among them as well – can now be explored in greater depth. However, before turning to this exploration in chapter 2's detailed study of three ways of studying gender, and of the complications that emerge when race and class are taken into account as well, more needs to be said about the character of prejudice itself. For, despite all the obvious differences that separate these forms of discrimination, several similar questions can and should be asked about gender bias, racial hatred, discrimination against lesbians and gays and/or a variety of other groups (fragmented and not): from where does discrimination emerge at all? Why do human beings engage in behaviors that can be exclusionary at best and genocidal at worst in the course of expressing express their dislike of "others"? And what have different theoretical traditions told us about this, if anything? While we will return to this profoundly important query in later chapters, and in this book's conclusion, a brief preview of several possible responses is offered preliminarily as a way of grounding later discussions.

One might say that prejudice has and can be explained within five traditions that have conceived bias in terms of (a) biology; (b) Freudian or psychologically oriented propensities; (c) Durkheimian ideas; (d) Marxist ideas; and (e) notions that merge the sociological and the psychological. Biological perspectives, like much of sociobiology itself, tend to offer rather simple and one-dimensional explanations of bias: in work on aggression like that written by Konrad Lorenz, discrimination is conceived as simply part of people's biological wiring.[9] Evolutionary theories also contain this leaning; while writers have differed in the exact physical causes to which they attribute aggression, they share a tendency to believe that some acting out of hostility between human beings is innate and biologically based. In this respect, again, these theories can be said to exemplify essentialism insofar as they can have a deterministic character.

While psychological theories move away from biological determinism to some extent, an element of inevitability remains in some of Sigmund Freud's writing, applicable to probing this fundamental question of commonalities: why prejudice? In *Civilization and Its Discontents*, Freud presumed that the very character of civilization made it virtually impossible that hatred between groups would not erupt from time to time in history.[10] Depressed at the time of its writing, and depressing in turn, *Civilization* makes war itself sound rather inevitable and unavoidable. This is because the two drives that Freud believes to be intrinsic to the human psyche – libido/eros and aggression/thanatos – cannot be fully expressed as societies develop. On the contrary, for civilization to emerge, Freud argued, drives must be redirected away from their primary direct expression into higher cultural pursuits. In Freud's terms sublimation, or the rechanneling of energy from drives' original objects into constructive social channels – finding cures for disease, making policies that try to end war, art, music, the writing of literature – must take place for civilization to be even conceivable. Consequently, in a Freudian framework, desires to express angry prejudices may always exist beneath the surface. Variable (and the only kernel of hope), though, is varied societies' abilities to teach its members to redirect their feelings – to learn, in other words, not to hate or exclude.

The third and fourth theories are more sociological in character. Rather than involving biological nature or psychic natures – and, therefore, unlike both of the first two theories' tendencies to propound essentialistic causes of prejudices – social practices that can be grasped and changed are seen to be at the source of human prejudices and biases. In the Durkheimian tradition, one that has given birth to moral panic theories in Britain and to Mertonian theories in the United States, groups may seek definition for themselves in opposition to "others" created for this very purpose. Thus Emile Durkheim argued in *The Rules of Sociological Method*, in the course of showing how what he called normal social processes can be distinguished from so-called pathological ones, that crime was actually functional for society.[11] No society has been free of some form of crime – by which Durkheim meant laws and taboos that separate law-abiding parties from transgressing ones – rendering crime itself paradoxically "normal" rather than "pathological." But why exactly, to Durkheim, was crime functional and normal? For Durkheim, defining someone as the other, the criminal, the law-breaker, is utterly necessary for people to see themselves as non-criminal and law-abiding by contrast.

In this tradition, then, social biases and prejudices have been used by societies and subgroups within them to create cohesion. Rather than this being inevitable, though, Durkheim saw his own role as a sociologist as bringing a certain amount of social reflexivity into being. To the extent that people become aware that "folk devils" (as British sociologist Stan Cohen described the process of creating "others" in *Folk Devils and Moral Panics*[12]) may often be socially constructed rather than intrinsically problematic, the need for such devils – and the function they serve – may wither accordingly.

Influential and powerful as this particular theory has been, Marxist explanations of bias are also important and relevant in offering another distinctly sociological interpretation. While Marx did not write in very much detail about bias and prejudice, it is easy to extrapolate from the body of his and Engels' ideas overall that prejudice may arise in the context of capitalist processes and dynamics. Thus, as some writers have noted in a post-Marxist vein, divisions between groups can serve a divide-and-conquer purpose. Take the United States as example: to the extent that the American working class focuses on racial and ethnic divisions among itself, so people are much less likely to notice the inordinate commonalities they/we share as workers. In this respect, Marx may have also implicitly suggested that prejudices of various kinds serve a purpose for capitalism in maintaining economic inequalities. (As we will see later, though, other writers and scholars may criticize this view as reductionistic, inclined toward reducing the complexities of race to a one-dimensional function of class.) Then, too, Marxist theory holds that a reserve army of labor – a group of workers who are under- or unemployed, and therefore desperate to take any job that arises even in strike-breaking situations – is crucial for capitalism's ability to maintain an upper hand over workers as a whole. This characteristic of capitalism may also foment various prejudices and hatred – not only racial and ethnically oriented but gender-aimed as well – that arise when some groups of workers become angered at other groups (rather than at the system) for accepting low wages and devaluing their own value as laborers.

Last but not least are theories that seek to combine aspects of individually oriented explanations (including but not limited to psychoanalytic ones) with distinctively sociological perspectives. For instance, one could apply Jack Katz's *Seductions of Crime* to understanding prejudices by combining Katz's interest in phenomenological influences (which he believes occur in the foreground of social situations) with classical sociological dimensions like gender, race, and class (that he knows loom in the background of people's lives).[13] Thus, even if capitalism sets people up to dislike others on supposedly racial or ethnic grounds, not every person will respond equally to that structural influence: individual differences may play out in vastly variable ways according to dynamically changing situations that are indeed existential in character.

Another psychosocial theory is one that flows from my book *Sadomasochism in Everyday Life* in which I tried to define sadomasochism as a simultaneously individual and collective dynamic emergent in a host of social settings from the bedroom to the boardroom. I argue that certain kinds of biases emerge in sadomasochistic cultures like our own as a result of both psychic and social influences.[14]

We will return to these and other theories in much more detail in chapters to come. Suffice it for now to say, though, that simply introducing the study of gender, race, and class was impossible without tapping a host of intellectual traditions and attempting – even preliminarily – to integrate them at the same time we also respect and incorporate their special differences. This intellectual challenge not only continues but deepens, becoming richer and more varied, as we move first to defining gender, then race, and (last but not at all least) class.

Lynn S. Chancer

CHAPTER TWO

Gender Defined and Refined

The term "gender" is by now used so frequently in academic discussions and popular references that one wonders whether students in particular, and the public in general, take for granted what it means. Of course, the meaning of gender is likely to vary depending on the context where it is used. Thus, to provide an overview, this chapter concentrates on providing three related but distinctive ways of defining gender in different interpretive traditions: sociologically, anthropologically, and historically.

In defining gender historically, it should be acknowledged at the outset that the term does not have a constant and invariant set of associations or meanings. Instead, one can view gender as a group of ideas, some of which theorists have agreed upon for decades and others which have been evolving, that grew out of and unfolded through a broad social movement concerned with women's (and men's) freedoms. Indeed, the feminist movement spawned the development of different "feminisms" from the 1970s through the present. Literally and figuratively, the movement has moved, changing and growing over the course of the last decades both in the United States and elsewhere. Through this process, the question "How do gender, race, and class interrelate?" generated courses and texts precisely like this one. A transition can thus be made rather seamlessly from defining gender in the first part of this chapter (especially through a historically oriented definition) to refining gender in its latter half. As we proceed, the conceptual vocabulary introduced in chapter 1 will also provide useful, and increasingly familiar, signposts.

Defining Gender Sociologically: from Sex to Social Construction

Of the three approaches, defining gender sociologically may be the clearest and easiest to grasp through examples based on people's everyday experiences.

Many introductory Women's Studies classes begin with a simple but solid sociological approach, differentiating "sex" and "gender" to clarify the meaning of each. "Sex" is said to refer primarily to anatomical distinctions between women and men made at birth; it is a term of biology, of physiology, that is arguably neutral. As with other kinds of physically based differences (brown hair as opposed to red, tall in height as opposed to short) reporting that someone is "male" or "female" need not, in and of itself, have cultural repercussions. Gender, on the other hand, refers to interpretations that have been socially constructed to skew the arguably "neutral" facts of gender in one evaluative direction or another. As Simone de Beauvoir writes in the first chapter of *The Second Sex*, the "facts of biology" cannot explain the universe of distinctions that came, over the course of history and convention, to block women's access to equal participation in all human endeavors. She contended that one was not born, but rather becomes a woman.[1]

Thus, gender refers to social and cultural interpretations that turn sexual difference into more than a merely biological distinction. Further, one can argue that "sex" has social repercussions only because of "gender"; it is on the basis of the latter that the worlds and activities of women, as opposed to those of men, have historically been demeaned. Thus, when teaching these terms, one can use the following simple schema:

SEX   GENDER
Male/Female   Masculine/Feminine

To further illustrate the enormity of gendered social constructions, I have often asked students what first comes into their minds when they hear the terms "masculine" and "feminine." This process of free association produces conventionally gendered images more often than one might imagine given the influence of the feminist movement from the 1970s through the present. Many students have said that they associate masculinity with toughness, strength, sports like playing football, the color blue, and sometimes, reflecting cultural changes, with unflattering terms like insensitivity and machismo. Femininity often continues to evoke opposite associations like delicate, passive, pretty, the color pink, and sometimes quite positive associations with the qualities of being caring, emotional, and nice.[2]

Answers to another experientially based question have similarly attested to the ongoing influence of gender. I have often asked my students what is the first thing people regularly ask when they hear that a new baby has been born. While someone might in theory inquire "How much did the baby weigh?" or "Is the baby healthy?," it is much more likely that most people will immediately inquire as to whether an infant is a boy or a girl. This suggests that gender takes on what sociologist of deviance Edwin Lemert has called a "primary status"; it trumps all other possible observations one could make about a given social phenomenon.[3] Another example of this ensues upon imagining that someone has referred to a person as a "lady" doctor or a "lady" cab driver. Why is it that gender mattered more than other possible attributes one might alternatively have remarked upon about this doctor or driver?

Probing further, defining gender sociologically also means noting that the two-sided bifurcations that have differentiated the worlds of "masculinity" and "femininity" have also, throughout most recorded history, accorded superiority to the former and inferiority to the latter. It is precisely such distinctions between "primary" and "secondary" that de Beauvoir's *The Second Sex* set out to explore.[4] But what, more precisely, has the enculturation of gender from early childhood bequeathed? According to de Beauvoir, within a traditional nuclear family in which a mother disproportionately parents and a father is deemed the breadwinner, little girls may initially seem to be the privileged ones because they are allowed to stay close to their mothers' skirts; they can continue to be clingy and emotional, and to express feelings of dependency if they wish to.[5] On the other hand, while the little girl is allowed this leeway, little boys soon learn that "to be a man" is to exude independence; as de Beauvoir describes, clearly drawing on a conventional model of familial expectations, little boys soon realize that their crying may be frowned upon.

Yet even if initially disadvantaged, de Beauvoir contends, boys also quickly begin to perceive that their sacrifice will be compensated; it will gradually be replaced by a patriarchally based sense of power and privilege. Indeed, according to de Beauvoir, the little boy gradually renounces the domestic realm with which women have historically been associated and embraces the public realm of men, sensing that this is a reservoir of eventual social and economic power.[6] Thus, gender comes to be associated not merely with a set of bifurcated characteristics that have been deeply engrained but with an entire universe that has been divided into separate but unequal spheres. These spheres extend beyond character traits to material realms with which "masculinity" and "femininity" have been linked, as illustrated by this second simple schema of traditional gendered dichotomies suggested below:

TRADITIONAL GENDER DICHOTOMIES
Masculinity	Femininity
Rationality	Emotionality

Activity	Passivity
Public	Private
Business	Family/Domesticity

Occupational ramifications:

Business	Retail sales, service and clerical jobs, elementary school teachers, caregivers
Politicians, lawyers	Secretaries, administrative assistants
Doctors/dentists	Nurses/dental assistants, home health aides

Crucial to note is that, in many societies including the United States, the realm of family and care-giving with which women have been associated has historically been devalued. Therefore, not surprisingly, gendered distinctions that have conventionally assigned women a disproportionate role within the family (and in child-rearing) have been transmuted into occupational distinctions as well.[7] For instance, empirical evidence in the US continues to show that women make only 70 cents to every $1.00 earned by men, this being an improvement. Between 1950 and 1980 the figure was only 60 cents to every $1.00.[8]

Probing further, gender-based differences in the realms that women traditionally occupy also explain their over-representation in care-giving professions: child-care, care for the elderly, secretarial (or administrative assistant work), nursing and elementary school teaching, among others. Moreover, studies of societies outside the United States also illustrate de Beauvoir's assertion that spheres associated with femininity have historically been accorded demeaned social status. Take Russia where, for decades, women have been doctors in much higher proportions; yet, in contrast to the US where this profession has long been male-dominated and extremely lucrative, they earn much lower pay. In US medicine, too, the pervasiveness of gender has manifested itself in a disproportionate number of women becoming pediatricians (reflecting, it would seem, traditional associations of femininity with the family and domesticity) whereas surgeons – by many thought to be the most prestigious sub-speciality of all, bringing high pay and involving responsibility for life and death – is still disproportionately comprised of men.[9]

Striking, too, is that even in fields that have historically been dominated by women one finds that men earn higher pay and occupy more prestigious entry-level posts. Consider cooking: due to its association with the domestic realm, this has conventionally been the province of women. However, in professional cooking, men hold higher positions as the most highly paid and visible representatives of this field. For example, France is well known for its red Michelin guide that rates chefs on a one- to three-star basis; a three-star rating is prestigious indeed, and usually bodes well for that restaurant's ability to sustain itself financially. Yet even in 2005, as these words are being written, a relatively "liberated" country like France still does not have a single woman who is a three-star chef. Likewise in many Western countries, including France and the United States, the teaching profession has tended to be quite male-dominated at its upper levels. Thus tenured university professors – arguably the highest paid group of teachers – remain, here and abroad, a group that is disproportionately comprised of men. On the other hand, women tend to be concentrated in elementary school teaching (as stems from traditional associations between women and domesticity).

Health-care workers? Again, the pattern applies. Take, for instance, an extremely low-paying type of work: taking care of the elderly who are homebound or in nursing homes. In general, few men work as home care attendants or as nursing home aides. But, when it comes to nursing home ownership or management (a highly profitable enterprise), men are disproportionately likely to be in charge. By no means should this be taken to obfuscate another important observation, however. In the contemporary United States, more and more women have begun to cross the gendered divide into more prestigious and traditionally male-dominated professions; statistics show that just about half the number of lawyers and doctors entering professional schools in these areas are women. Yet, the numbers are hardly analogous when we look at the number of men who have entered occupations historically dominated by women.[10] Thus, while women are becoming lawyers, doctors, business people, and/or entering politics, far fewer numbers of men have shown an interest in becoming nurses. Popular cultural representations – like the amusing American movie *Meet the Parents* that features Robert De Niro playing a retired military man initially horrified when his daughter brings home her fiancé who is a nurse (played by Ben Stiller) – suggest that changes in older gendered presumptions may be slowly occurring. Yet, statistically speaking, more women have entered traditionally male-dominated professions than the other way around. Why?

One reason is obvious: male-dominated fields, from medicine to business, are high-paying. On the other hand, jobs like day-care center workers or nursing home workers – occupied in disproportionate numbers by women – have not been well paid. As feminist legal scholar Martha Fineman has argued, this suggests that deeply engrained notions about the social value (or lack thereof) of care-giving would have to change for undervalued occupations like nursing or working with children to attract both men and women in equal numbers.[11]

A second reason is that, were they to enter traditionally female occupations, men might feel as though their "masculinity" (again, defined in conventionally gendered terms) was being subtly, or not so subtly, impugned. Even in 2005, when much about our attitudes toward gender have changed, a male entering the field of nursing may feel as though at risk of seeming "effeminate." Consequently, for men, crossing gendered lines may bring negative consequences that are not only sexist but also heterosexist, revealing biases against people who are gay and who do not pursue work traditionally associated with masculinity. In this respect, the gendered dichotomies described so thoroughly by de Beauvoir are enacted in a world that has not only mandated the separation of masculinity and femininity (demeaning the latter in favor of the former) but has dictated sexual norms as well (that is, of course, heterosexuality).

Thus defining gender sociologically means distinguishing between "gender" and "sex" and understanding the immensity of implications that arise once masculinity and femininity have been socially constructed in a world of binary oppositions. Suzanne J. Kessler and Wendy McKenna's work on transsexualism which laid the groundwork for Queer Studies, argues that "It may be easier today to see that particular individuals have both masculine and feminine features, but we still treat gender as dichotomous and most certainly treat sex that way."[12] Interestingly, in the work of Judith Butler, this very "dichotomy" itself is called into question as gendered at its core.[13] Thus, Butler criticizes de Beauvoir and other feminist writings and courses influenced by her thinking for failing to analyze how the use of gendered binaries like "femininity" and "masculinity" keeps these distinctions alive (rather than, as initially hoped for by feminists, contributing to the obsolescence of these categories). In effect, as Butler suggests, binary categories in and of themselves provide a linguistic vehicle through which "women," among others, come to be maintained as "others." In a classic paper entitled "Doing Gender" that likewise calls attention to the purposefully created rather than intrinsically dualistic character of gender, Candace West and Don Zimmerman contend that "Doing gender involves a complex of socially guided perceptual, interactional, and micropolitical activities that cast particular pursuits as expressions of masculine and feminine 'natures.'"[14]

We will come back to debates in gender, race, and class that have questioned the very language that is used to depict the identities of diverse groups – women, racial and ethnic minorities, gays and lesbians – who have encountered a range of social biases. For now, though, let us turn to defining gender in a second way that centers on the following issue: if women have been historically constructed as the "second sex," why has this happened? What are some well-known theories that have been offered to explain the evolution of this problem over so many decades, indeed centuries?

Defining Gender Anthropologically:
Why "the Second Sex"?

Two theories have been particularly influential in attempting to explain why "the second sex," and by extension gendered divisions, developed historically. The first was presented in a well-known article written by Columbia University anthropologist Sherri Ortner. The second, based on weaker and much debated anthropological evidence, is nevertheless worth exploring because of its sway on the unfolding of the American feminist movement. This is the theory of gender's origins found in Frederick Engels' *The Origin of the Family, Private Property and the State*.

In the essay "Is Female to Male as Nature is to Culture?" Ortner presented the ensuing thesis.[15] According to Ortner's interpretation of the available anthropological evidence, all known societies have made a basic distinction between nature and culture that comes to be associated with a corresponding bifurcation between femininity and masculinity. Ortner's now well-known article states that a universal goal of virtually all known human societies is to value life over death. Human beings seek to transcend our mortality through activities, innovations, and aspirations that aim at distancing us from our otherwise inevitable demise. Thus, for example, societies greatly value the discovery of a vaccination that can cure a disease or the completion of a huge project – a building, perhaps, or a work of literature – that impresses upon us our ability to defy nature and live on indefinitely. All this, Ortner contends, has been linked with the world of "culture" that purposively overcomes the uncertainties of "nature."

As societies seek to transcend and dominate the world of nature, Ortner argues, women are placed at a disadvantage because they are associated with the natural world. Women's biological role in the reproduction of the species through childbearing and lactation has been connected with cyclical, often messy aspects of nature that ebb and flow in contrast to linear processes that seem much more one-directional and predictable. Not surprisingly, natural processes are also associated with the uncertainties of death and mortality. These associations may explain both why women have been kept within the domestic realm and why care-giving work has historically been demeaned. In short, women's historical subordination parallels the historical subordination of nature to culture.

While Ortner's argument is certainly a provocative one, it contains an analytic flaw. It is not inevitable that we view the world of culture as separable from, or superior to, the world of nature. Alternatively, one could argue that culture and nature are inextricably linked. Take, for example, the sphere of scientific development and experimentation. Men have been disproportionately represented (and women have often been discriminated against) in the world of science. But, arguably, scientific activities involve both culture and nature. Biologists, chemists, and physicists obviously work in and with the natural world; moreover, it is the character of experimentation to partake of cyclical as well as linear processes.

Secondly, even if nature and culture could be neatly separated in principle, Ortner's explanation about according inferiority to the former and superiority to the latter does not account for why other conceivable interpretations did not emerge. For instance, why wouldn't some clans, societies, or tribes conclude that both nature and culture are necessary for human beings to survive and flourish, leading their members to surmise that both should be accorded approximately equal worship, respect, and value? Consequently, while Ortner's theory is significant, further exploration of why and how women came to be deemed "the second sex" is needed.

Here, one can turn to an older theory that has been highly influential (especially in terms of the evolution of feminisms as discussed below) despite its being based on anthropological evidence considered more out-dated than Ortner's.[16] Frederick Engels' *The Origin of the Family, Private Property, and the State* is the only major work within the Marxist lexicon of ideas that focuses on the genesis of women's oppression within the trad-itional nuclear family.[17] Given the close relationship of Marx and Engels, this volume is frequently taken to represent the thought of both on gender and family-related matters. According to Engels, drawing on anthropolo-gist Lewis Henry Morgan's work, it is not correct to say that most early clans and tribes devalued women.[18] Rather, many early societies were organized matriarchally (that is, women held major positions of power) or were matrilineal (that is, property passed down in the women's line). Moreover, against the notion that associations with nature led to their devaluation, Engels suggested that at earlier points some societies have worshipped and been awestruck by women's biologically based capacity for reproduction. This suggests that, at earlier points in human history, male/female relations may have been more harmonious than the relatively conflictual image one is left with by an anthropological theory like Ortner's.

However, note that while Engels disputes that women's secondary status always existed, he does allow that human activities were broken down into separate spheres on the basis of gender. Men were involved in hunting activities that took them outside the domestic center of the tribe whereas women were involved with gathering foodstuffs and the preparing of meals, child-rearing, and craft-related activities. Thus Engels, like Ortner, recognized the longstanding persistence of male-dominated as opposed to female-dominated realms. Unlike Ortner's, though, Engels' account is distinctive in contending that women's status in the domestic realm was initially equal if not superior to that of men.

When did this harmonious situation change? According to Engels, the beginning of women's oppressed status coincided and grew gradually alongside the development in human history of private property relations. Why? One reason is that surplus arose in the hunting rather than the domestic sphere of human activities. Once a given tribe, clan, or group began producing more than it actually needed to sustain and reproduce itself, an embryonic form of private property developed. Moreover, because surplus developed in the sphere of activity that was dominated by men, the problem arose of how to identify who was a legitimate heir.[19] For, unless a woman was monogamous, one could not establish the actual paternity of a child; on the other hand, a man could have sexual relations with multiple women so long as he had a "lawful" wife.

With this, argued Engels, came double standards of sexuality that have been part and parcel of women's subordination from the rise of capitalism until now. It became commonplace for men to have several sexual partners, whereas women with more than a single partner out of wedlock were socially shunned. An interesting ramification of Engels' theory is that it offers an explanation for when and how divisions between so-called good and bad women, virgins and whores, came into being. Engels suggests that, with the emergence of private property, women became a form of property and often carried dowries along with them; they would be traded between tribes and possessed few, if any, rights of their own. Thus the institutionalization of monogamous marriage transformed intimate sexual relationships into opportunities for accumulation, much to the detriment of women.

Engels' theory also has the advantage of offering an explanation for why the ability of women to gain credit or to divorce on their own, without permission from husbands, was delayed until relatively recently in Western civilization's history. Even in the United States, where women's rights have grown over the last century and where legislation now prohibits gender discrimination, Engels' theory has contemporary significance, particularly with respect to ongoing vestiges of attitudes toward marital rape. Husbands cannot be prosecuted for raping their wives in Kentucky, Missouri, New Mexico, North Carolina, Oklahoma, South Carolina, South Dakota, or Utah unless they live apart or are legally separated, have already filed for divorce, or have an order of protection.[20] In twenty-six other states, exemptions to marital rape prosecutions that are not applicable to non-marital rape prosecutions still exist. These laws tend to confirm Engels' argument. Indeed, as Carole Pateman explains in *The Sexual Contract*, marriage laws have viewed women as men's property (recall the unequal pronouncement in traditional marriage ceremonies: I now pronounce you "man and wife").[21] Applied thereafter to rape, as Diana Russell discusses in *Rape in Marriage*, how is it possible to rape someone whom one owns, who is one's property?

What is important to underscore about Engel's theory, then, is both its ongoing explanatory resonance – especially in parts of the world where women still lack legal rights and are indeed considered sexual property (for example, in a number of Middle Eastern and African countries, women can be stoned to death if found engaging in adultery) – and the relationship between the theory and its conclusions. Clearly, Engels' theory has prescriptive implications for liberating women. For if the origins of women's oppression lies in private property relations and the institutionalization of a rigidly monogamous nuclear family, then "liberation" must necessitate overcoming private property in order to realize freedom (as well as freer choices within women's sexual and intimate relationships). By extension, it follows that socialism rather than capitalism should be in the interest of women's liberation. Thus, this perspective from Marx and Engels has the analytic virtue of offering not only a critique but also a corresponding solution. Socialism would bring women, as workers, out of the domestic into the public sphere, allowing them to achieve economic independence denied them within the confines of the nuclear family.

But, as with Ortner's theory, there are also flaws in Engels' interpretation. If we return to the latter's theory of how women's secondary status arose, at least three pitfalls in logic come to mind. For one thing, according to Engel's portrayal, why did surplus emerge only in the sphere of hunting and gathering where men worked rather than also through domestic activities with which women were engaged? There is no particular reason why women's labor would not also have produced surplus goods that other tribes might wish to acquire. Secondly, even if this were factually the case – and surplus emerged only from men's laboring activities – why wasn't this surplus shared equally between men and women? Why did men and not women need to establish an heir? This query seems especially germane when, according to Engels (and Morgan), men and women existed in an idyllic and communal state prior to the emergence of private property; if this were so, it ought not to have mattered where surplus arose. Still a third problem exists. Engels' theory presumes that men and women willingly agreed to divide their activities into well-defined separate spheres. But again, if all was actually harmonious between the sexes centuries ago, prior to the development of private property and capitalism, why wouldn't men sometimes decide to stay at home and engage in so-called women's work? Conversely, why wouldn't women sometimes decide to engage in the hunting and gathering activities with which men were disproportionately involved? One immediate response might be biologically based, namely, that women stayed close to the domestic hearth because of their role in reproduction and indeed with "nature": females may have often been pregnant and thus unable to engage in the same activities as men. But surely women were not pregnant all the time: if permitted, a range of women (from teenagers through post-menopausal in age) might well have wished to partake in traditionally male expeditions outside the limited domestic sphere. Why didn't they?

With this, we return to Engel's analysis of "why" women came to be oppressed and to a third way of defining gender – namely, through the history of feminism(s) as part of a broad and influential social movement. For one way of addressing the shortcomings of Engels' argument is to posit that gendered relations prior to the development of private property were not as ideal as assumed. It may have been that the apparently well-defined division between domestic and hunting spheres was not the product of communally agreed-upon, separate but equal, arrangements at all. Rather, the divide may have reflected gendered relations of power between men and women already in existence; another way of stating this is that a distinctly gendered class system may have antedated the rise of private property. Moreover, a gendered division of power between men and women may have itself emerged not voluntarily but on the basis of force.[22] Indeed, borrowing Marx's and Engel's language, perhaps the materialist basis of a gendered class system in early human history was that women's role in reproduction and men's greater physical strength made it possible for men to dominate them coercively, forcing rather than persuading women to accept confinement to domestic realms of activity that became devalued in the worth accorded them.

This analysis explains the flaws in Engels' argument above. Even if surplus emerged in women's realms of activities, it would have been appropriated by men (this comprising an earlier form of appropriation than that of capitalists, the main form of appropriation with which Marx and Engels were concerned). Also explained through the hypothesis of a prior gender-class system is men's failure to share surplus equally with women (that is, this not being in the interests of maintaining power as a male-dominated group), and women's failure to participate equally in both natural and cultural domains of human labor (that is, this was not a viable option).

Interestingly, this critique also provides some insight into the related deficiency in Ortner's argument pinpointed earlier. Nature and culture may also not have been democratically agreed-upon divisions, nor may women have voluntarily accepted the higher valuation of the former relative to the latter. Again, as Susan Brownmiller has argued, coercion may have been involved and facilitated by dint of biological differences in physical strength.

Indeed, as we will see below, it is precisely this argument that is at the heart of a famous piece of radical feminist theory. Shulamith Firestone began her now well-known *The Dialectic of Sex* by criticizing Engels on similar grounds to those just explicated. According to Firestone, a "sex class" system preceded the economic class system about which Marx and Engels were concerned. This did not mean that Firestone as a radical thinker did not also oppose capitalism. Instead, for Firestone, the most basic form of power relationship was marriage insofar as inequality between the sexes had become institutionalized in the gender-biased laws that favored monogamous nuclear families. By extension, she questioned whether eliminating capitalism would simultaneously lead to the collapse of patriarchy and the domination of men by women. No doubt improving women's economic situation would help. Yet flowing from Firestone's analysis is the possibility that, unless gender-based oppression in the family was addressed at its core, women might find themselves subordinated within the home even if they were relatively freer at the workplace. Prescient here was that *The Dialectic of Sex* foretold what actually happened with the rise in many Communist societies of the twentieth century such as the Soviet Union or Yugoslavia. Although women's economic situation as workers improved, they often found themselves doing double labor, or second shifts, that is, having to shoulder a disproportionate share of house-cleaning and child-care responsibilities.[23]

While Firestone also suggested that force may have been at the basis of this pre-capitalistic "sex class" system, she did not envision this system's survival as inevitable or even probable. Consequently, insofar as it holds out possibilities of future change, her theory was analogous to that of Marx and Engels. As technology became more and more sophisticated and refined, Firestone contended that the areas of gender, power, and biology would become less closely related. Wars waged through the use of nuclear armaments require pushing buttons, not pumping iron; for this reason, Firestone's theory held that there was a materialist basis for believing that feminist-based transformations would be the wave of the future.

But before turning in greater detail to analyzing the pros and cons of radical feminist arguments as exemplified by Firestone and others, let us turn more systematically to the evolution of gender and its relationship to other dimensions of the social world as seen through the lens of unfolding feminisms.

Defining Gender Historically: the Social Movement of Feminisms

From the 1970s to the present, more varieties of feminist perspectives have appeared on the American cultural landscape than can easily be named. From poststructural to psychoanalytic, liberal to radical, Marxist to social-ist, ecological to cultural feminisms, the sheer scope of ideas and theories that feminist theorists and activists have produced attest to a movement that remains lively, impassioned, and engaged. By 2005, feminists in the United States are also more aware than ever of the international character of the women's movement.[24] For instance, an important international conferences on women's rights that was held in India in late 2004 drew hundreds of participants from the United States, highly committed to placing questions of women's freedom (or lack thereof) in a global context. Indeed, Peggy Antrobus refers to a developing global women's movement in describing an emerging set of commonalities over issues like inter-national corporate power and the need to eradicate poverty, at the same time as wide differences between women (of class, race, sexuality, age, nation, to name only a few) still pertain.[25] Where, then, to begin a summary of how this rich and complicated history of feminisms has gone hand in hand with evolving understandings of gender?

In order to narrow down an otherwise enormous task, the following remarks focus predominantly on the history of second-wave feminism in a specifically US context. This said, we will also be focusing on a subset of feminist ideas that have played a disproportionately important role in shaping and reshaping what now seem to be widely accepted interpret-ations of gender. With the US context in mind, let us turn to a discussion of (1) liberal feminism; (2) radical feminism (and its relationship to cultural and ecological feminism); (3) Marxist feminism; (4) socialist feminism; and (5) black feminist thought. In each of the short sections below, we provide examples of major texts and feminist thinkers associated with the various feminist perspectives before turning to main ideas that can be culled from each perspective. One small caveat is in order here, though: we are not pretending to cover any and all brands of feminist thinking. For instance, authors whose writings could be grouped under the headings "psychoanalytic feminism" or "poststructural feminism" are not considered in depth. The feminisms we do consider often reflect the ideas of organized groups of feminists rather than intellectual currents within feminism (although the latter have, no doubt, also been important in feminisms' historical development overall). Last but not least, we conclude each section's brief discussion of these types of feminisms by showing how criticisms made of each may have spurred ideas (some corrective in character) that other feminisms have elaborated. An important consequence of this evolution is that it underscores how, based on this third and final way of defining gender, interest in gender, race, and class as a subject matter emerged.

Divisions between Marxist and socialist feminists and liberal and radical feminists can be said to have centered on class divisions between women. Black feminist thought certainly developed when important activists and writers such as Bell Hooks, Michelle Wallace, and (in sociology) Patricia Hill Collins criticized feminism for giving short shrift to racial differences between women. At that point, this chapter's second goal – not only reviewing how gender can be defined but how it came to be refined – can, hopefully, be fulfilled.

I   Liberal feminism

Mirroring its name, liberal feminism harks back to the Enlightenment idea of liberalism itself. Following the French and American Revolutions, and rebelling against the restrictions of feudalism, philosophers of the Enlightenment stressed rights believed to accrue to a newly emerging "individual": central among these were voting rights and rights related to ownership of property. While most philosophers of the time did not critically examine who was included or excluded under the umbrella of individual rights, John Stuart Mill (and, as belatedly acknowledged, Harriet Taylor Mill) co-authored *The Subjection of Women* to make the following case.[26] According to John Stuart Mill and Harriet Taylor Mill, liberalism was poorly served by any definition of individual rights that failed to include women. Such exclusion kept half of humanity, and therefore large numbers of women, from participating in the development and enrichment of society. Mary Wollstonecraft made a similar argument in *A Vindication of the Rights of Women* (1790), showing that liberal feminism has roots that go as far back as the eighteenth century.[27]

Indeed, in the American context, what has been called the "first wave" of feminism – born when women involved in the abolitionist movement realized that they, too, did not possess basic rights – emphasized the goal of enfranchising women. Feminists like Lucy Stone, Susan B. Anthony, and Elizabeth Cady Stanton participated in what could therefore be called, in this regard, early liberal feminist activism. But it was not until the 1970s, when second-wave feminism exploded onto the 1960s social movement scene with impassioned new writings, and small and large groups engaged with feminist issues, that the term "liberal feminism" started to be associated more clearly with particular activists and their books and ideas.

In particular, Betty Friedan's *The Feminine Mystique* gave voice to many women's previously inchoate longings to move out of household and domestic confinement, and to participate in "an equal partnership of the sexes."[28] Not surprisingly, Friedan became the first president of the National Organization of Women, formed in 1966, as the quintessential organizational embodiment of second-wave liberal feminism in the United States.[29] The National Organization of Women (NOW) soon made inroads into a wide range of arenas from which women had been traditionally excluded, and took on myriad issues of which a common denominator was inequality. Pay disparities, occupational segregation, workplace discrimination, child-care, education, and marriage and divorce were among the many areas with which liberal feminists became involved. In the 1970s, too, liberal feminist energies resulted in the introduction of the Equal Rights Amendment (ERA), a constitutional amendment aimed at prohibiting gender discrimination of any kind.[30] The amendment, submitted to the states in 1972, initially passed in thirty-five states and appeared to be headed for passage. However, a decade later, as the deadline for ratification expired, the struggle to secure the three additional votes necessary to pass the amendment, continued.[31] Ultimately the amendment failed because of opponents' highly publicized concerns that ERA meant an erosion of women's rights and protections, including the right to child support and alimony after divorce and wartime draft and combat exemption.[32] Despite this defeat, the liberal feminist spirit found legislative expression in the passage of Title VII of the Civil Rights Act, specifically intended to forbid both gender- and race-based discrimination in any place of education or employment where federal monies were spent. Moreover, the liberal feminist slogan "Equal pay for equal work" little by little seeped into widespread cultural understandings. As women moved in massive numbers during these decades into workplaces (for example, into fire and police departments, law and medicine) from which they had traditionally been excluded, disparities originally noticeable between women's and men's pay became apparent and were subjected to criticism on liberal feminist grounds.[33]

What then, if anything, was problematic about liberal feminism? One criticism, expanded upon below, was that liberal feminism suffered from a problem similar to that which plagued liberalism in general. While ostensibly committed to universal-sounding notions of equality, in practice, its ideas were such that it protected only some individuals' rights. Whereas in the eighteenth century the term "individual" did not extend to women or men who did not own property, American liberal feminism has often been faulted for failing to take into account the problems and different experiences of women of color and women of diverse classes.[34] But since this criticism was also one directed against radical feminism, we turn now to how radical feminist ideas took issue with – and expanded upon – what were seen as limiting notions of liberal feminism. Radical feminists tended to be dissatisfied with the gendered division between public and private spheres that liberal feminism took for granted. The goal of liberal feminism, in theory as well as practice, was to move women from the domestic sphere within which they had been confined into the world of business, or culture (as Ortner, as explained earlier, referred to this latter term). Correspondingly, Friedan and others sought a world where women could hold any job they chose to in the valued public sphere.[35] But while this goal was certainly worthwhile, and though liberal feminism has been extraordinarily influential, radical feminists sought to explore the roots and repercussions of gender more deeply. Whereas the schema presented above separating masculinity and femininity is kept in place by liberal feminism, radical feminists sought to explode it for the following set of reasons.

2   Radical feminism

For radical feminists, the very division between nature and culture, public and private, that is at the heart of gender needed to be transformed: this was the source of women's subordination. Why, at base, did that dichotomy exist and persist? While US radical feminists of the 1970s and 1980s held different ideas on this subject, at least four core ideas can be identified to clarify why and how this type of feminism differs from the liberal variety. Key radical feminist texts referred to in the ensuing discussion are Kate Millett's *Sexual Politics*, Shulamith Firestone's *The Dialectic of Sex*, and Ti-Grace Atkinson's *Amazon Odyssey*.

(a) The concept of patriarchy

Well-known writings of early radical feminism, prominent among these Kate Millett's *Sexual Politics* and Shulamith Firestone's *The Dialectic of Sex*, frequently referred to "patriarchy" as a central concept. Perhaps one could say that the concept of patriarchy is to radical feminist theory what the concept of capitalism is to Marxist theory.[36] While the classical translation of this term is "law of the father," to Millett, it came to mean male domination in an institutional as well as cultural sense. To Millett and other radical feminist theorists, patriarchal societies were ones wherein, if examined closely, men held positions of power in virtually all decision-making spheres. For example, by this definition, a country is patriarchal if those who head its economy (businesses and corporations) are overwhelmingly male, and if this could also be said of those who hold power in the fields of technology and science, the military and police, governmental apparatuses, and even (as final decision-makers) in the home. At the time Millett wrote *Sexual Politics* in 1970, most countries – certainly including the United States – were patriarchal by this definition. By 2005, one could say that this has changed to some degree, though a strong case can still be made that most European and American nations (even where women heads of business can be pointed to, along with obvious increases in the numbers of women who are in politics) remain male-dominated. Many countries in the Middle East, Africa, Asia, and Latin America also leave little doubt that they are patriarchal by this definition. This brings us to a second major point of radical feminist theory, namely, that a key to patriarchal power, and to patriarchal justification of subordinating an entire sex, has been controls that are exercised over women's bodies and justified through cultural and/or religious ideologies of various kinds.

(b) The centrality of the body and sexuality to controls exerted over women

Radical feminists have typically pointed out that key to male-dominated societies are the controls they have exerted over women's bodies. Thus, according to Firestone, women were not confined to the domestic sphere willingly but coercively. Moreover, women's ability to control whether or not to have children, who to have sexual relations with and under what conditions, are matters that in patriarchal societies have been strictly limited. In many countries, women still face death for committing adultery, and double standards of sexual conduct are widely accepted.

In the United States, where liberal feminists characteristically took up the issue of the Equal Rights Amendment, radical feminists – just as tellingly – were initially engaged with the issue of abortion.[37] The importance of reproductive choice was intimately related, in practice, to the radical feminist belief, in theory, that control over women's bodies has been central to gender subordination. Consequently, ongoing efforts to defend the 1973 victory for reproductive rights symbolized in *Roe* v. *Wade* are consistent with the influence of this early basic idea – namely, that patriarchy remains powerful or becomes diminished to the extent that women are able to exert control over their own bodies. Indeed, a well-known early radical feminist text, *Our Bodies/Ourselves*, aimed at pragmatic assistance with this goal by offering how-to health and gynecological advice.[38]

(c) The personal is political

An aphorism that became well known and is often misunderstood, namely the notion of the personal as political, also stemmed from early radical feminist writing, in particular, from the very title of Kate Millett's book *Sexual Politics*.[39] Millet sought to expand the notion of politics from an older conception (that is, people often free-associate the word "politics" with elections, voting rights, and other matters that would be discussed in Political Science courses) to a far more extensive, indeed radical, understanding. To Millett and other radical feminists influenced by her writings, power relations that are indeed political are regularly enacted across a much wider spectrum of human activities and relationships. Thus, politics are not limited in their occurrence to traditionally masculine realms of business, work, and politics. Rather, political relationships occur on a daily basis in traditionally feminine spheres of activity, particularly in the domestic sphere and within nuclear families as well.

Not surprisingly, then, *Sexual Politics* – initially written to fulfill a PhD requirement in English at Columbia University – starts with scenes of sex that take place in bedrooms and kitchens, and draws on the novels of four well-known male authors (Norman Mailer, D. H. Lawrence, Jean Genet, and Henry Miller) to develop a radical feminist analysis. According to Millett, the novels of these four authors are routinely taught as "classics." Yet, many of these authors' books read as though they could be works of pornography, and sadomasochistic pornography at that. This was precisely Millett's point: "ordinary" sexual relations that take place in "everyday" relationships in the bedroom, and are made into literary art and endowed with cultural legitimacy, are steeped in gender-skewed depictions of dominance and subordination. In our culture, Millett argued, such "sexual politics" have been normalized. The importance of this analysis was that it suggested that a variety of relationships that occur in the home need to be thought of as political whether the power relations within them were understood as such (or not).

Thus, one accomplishment of radical feminist thought was to make clear that issues like domestic violence, rape (including rape in marriage), and sexual harassment were indeed instances of sexual politics. Prior to radical feminism, a theoretical basis may not have existed to understand these issues as such. For instance, if the police were called in a domestic violence case to break up a situation involuing battering, they might refuse to intervene on the ground that this was a private family matter. Yet, Millett's work and that of other radical feminists illuminated the extent to which so-called personal domination that occurs in the private sphere of domesticity was equally worthy of exposure and politicization.[40]

This also affected evaluations of men's behavior. As historian Sara Evans describes in *Personal Politics*, a fascinating chronicle of 1960s and 1970s feminist activism, some prominent New Left figures who were male – and who, on the one hand, were explicitly concerned about racial and class inequalities – were, on the other, known to treat women in offensively sexist ways.[41] But if "the personal is political" as radical feminists contended, then these men's apparently admirable qualities in the public sphere would be seriously undermined by calling attention to their chauvinism toward women. From this radical feminist expansion of the notion of politics beyond gender-dichotomized categories, the conclusion followed that it was not acceptable to uphold values in one sphere that were contradicted in another. Here, again, a long-term effect of American radical feminism may have been to provide theoretical underpinnings for cultural shifts in how high-profile events – for example, the sexual harassment case involving Clarence Thomas and Anita Hill, and even the impeachment of Bill Clinton over the Monica Lewinsky affair – came to be interpreted. For sexual harassment in the workplace, of which the Supreme Court nominee Clarence Thomas had been accused, was later perceived as suggesting that a person's improprieties in matters of sexual politics potentially affected his or her ability to serve in more traditionally understood political arenas as well. Similarly, negative reactions to President Clinton's relationship with Monica Lewinsky, and later accusations of sexual harassment raised by Paula Jones, illustrate that the radical feminist aphorism "the personal is political" had made its way, at least to some extent, into American cultural consciousness. A fourth point of radical feminist analysis takes us even closer than the others to how this type of feminist theory leads to one way of defining gender; this last observation is also particularly germane for distinguishing gender-related issues from race- and class-related ones.

(d) Internal colonization

Ti-Grace Atkinson was a well known and ultimately notorious figure in early radical feminist theory and activism. One reason for this notoriety was Atkinson's assertion that, because social controls exerted over women within patriarchal societies have been so enormous, women needed to form a "sex class" and attempt to overcome, apart from men, their historic subordination. At one point, Atkinson advocated women's living and organizing apart from men in a way that recalls the early Greek play *Lysistrata*.[42] While her work *Amazon Odyssey* may sometimes be overlooked for just this reason, it nevertheless offered what became another influential (if unattributed) insight.[43]

Atkinson contended that, once relationships between men and women were defined in terms of dominance and subordination and seen to comprise "sexual politics," another analytic distinction between this particular form of power and others also came into relief. Gender was the only form of dominance and subordination relationship that involved the more powerless person regularly, and as a matter of course, sleeping and having sexual relations with the less powerful one. This means that generating class consciousness on the basis of sex is likely to be rendered difficult indeed. One's ability to feel a sense of common cause with others in one's (sex) class is constantly being diluted by a sense of emotional and sexual intimacy that, as a matter of course, brings the subordinated party closer – and less likely to uncomfortably challenge – the dominated one.

Contrast this now with class-based and race-based forms of power, starting with the powerful/powerless relationship that exists between a capitalist and a worker. Let's imagine that the worker did not leave his or her job at the end of a work day but rather returned home with his/her boss to sleep and possibly have sex: how might this affect the possibilities of workers organizing as a group to overcome the subordination they experienced in terms of class? Atkinson's analysis suggests, not surprisingly, that sleeping with the empowered party was likely to dilute the worker's consciousness of his/her oppressed status, thereby making the task of workers' collective organizing more difficult.

But, in fact, this hypothetical situation is not what actually happens in the case of class-based subordination: as Marx described, contemporary capitalism brings workers together at the workplace, precisely where trade union organizing is likely to occur. Analogously in this respect, organizing against racial discrimination may have been facilitated (though, of course, unintentionally) by historical circumstances that sometimes allowed – or forced – people of the same race to live together. Thus organizing against South African apartheid might have been even more difficult, paradoxically, were it not for blacks having been forced to live together. Residential segregation may have unintentionally facilitated group-based organizing in a way that would have been more difficult under conditions where people facing a similar form of discrimination were separated from one another. Of course, one might counter-argue that gender is not distinctive from race-based discrimination in that, during American slavery, African American women often were separated from their families and endured sexual coercion (that is, rape) by plantation owners.[44] Yet, thankfully, analyzing the horrors of slavery is to call attention to an anomalous situation of impermanent historical duration. Atkinson was arguing, though, that gender-based relationships are distinctive – and, in this sense different from class and racially based power relationships – in that sexual and emotional intimacy occurring between the relatively powerful and relatively powerless parties is a "normal" rather than anomalous structural feature within them.

Consequently, according to radical feminist theorists like Atkinson and others, organizing against sexual subordination was the most difficult form of consciousness-raising to undertake – and, in this respect, possibly even more difficult than organizing against racial and class-based oppressions. Suggested by this analysis, too, is that sex-based organizing was something that would have to take place across different races, different ethnicities, different classes, and different regions. This is because *within* a particular race/ethnicity or class – whether among Hispanics or blacks or Italian Americans or Japanese Americans, or among the working class or the upper class – heterosexual couples, commonly divided by a gender-based difference of power and powerlessness between them, were likely to be found. Thus, gender oppression was likely to be a remarkably pervasive form that would not simply wither away once/if racial, and/or ethnic/ and/or class-based discriminations were eased. We will return to this point several times in ensuing chapters, both theoretically and in the course of providing concrete examples of how gender discrimination cannot be reduced to a function of race or class-based discriminations.

From this, it can be concluded that the content of early radical feminist ideas was both substantively rich and extraordinarily influential. Without these ideas, the cultural impact gender has had on modern societies, nationally and internationally, would not have been as enormous – nor, indeed, as radical. But then why, by 2005, is it also arguably as common to come across criticisms of radical feminism as much as tributes to it? Two substantive critiques of radical feminist theory now need to be identified especially since, separately and taken together, they elucidate why some women came to deem other types of feminisms more appealing and, as is even more salient, why concerns about the relationship between gender, race, and class emerged among many feminists.

The first now well-established critique of radical feminist theory brings us back to the concept of patriarchy and to the common conceptual vocabulary set out in chapter 1. For many feminists, a problem with radical feminist thought was its tendency to universalize patriarchy rather than to envision gender-based oppression in historically specific terms. According to critics, radical feminist accounts made it seem that patri- archy existed everywhere, in all prior and present times and places, uniformly. But did not the way women experienced patriarchy vary depending on, for instance, whether someone lived in the Soviet Union (amidst communist ideology that, at least in principle, promoted women's equality) or in Saudi Arabia (where women's rights in a modern sense did not exist)? Didn't it matter in defining patriarchy whether we focus on the experience in the United States of an independently wealthy woman (whose economic status meant that she could hire other women to do her own child-care and housework) or of a working-class woman whose financial situation did not allow such privileges?

A second frequent critique of radical feminism is at once related and separable. In common with liberal feminist theory, radical feminist theory came to be seen by other feminists – particularly Marxist feminists, social- ist feminists, and feminists of color – as oriented primarily toward the needs of middle- and upper-class white women. Its approach to gender was to advocate a sex-class politics supposedly in the interests of *all* women. Yet, this approach proceeded as though differences of class and race between women could blithely be overlooked or subsumed within the undifferentiated category of "women." Thus, radical feminists were accused of reductionism (presenting us with an example of how, in this volume, this term will recurrently come into play). In other words, according to feminists concerned about class and racial differences between women, radical feminist analyses tended to reduce class and race differences to a function of gender. Radical feminist theorists made it sound as though, if only gender-based subordination vanished, other actually existing differences between women – based on race, ethnicity, and/or class, sexual preference, to name several important sociological distinctions – would fade away correspondingly. But why would this be the case? For, as we are about to see, Marxist, socialist, and feminists of color did not believe the situation was so simple.

3 Marxist feminism

For Marxist feminists, gender was no doubt important but so were class-based differences between women. Indeed, Marxist feminist thinkers felt that economic problems faced by women were central to maintaining their dependent and subordinate status.[45] For most feminists taking this approach, little or no change was possible unless women came closer to achieving economic parity with men. Not surprisingly, given this theoretical orientation, Marxist feminist analyses were more likely to advocate social movement organizing around bread-and-butter economic issues. Through the 1970s and 1980s, two issues in particular interested Marxist feminists, and are worth mentioning.

One issue of concern to Marxist feminists in the 1970s involved "wages for housework" campaigns.[46] Juliet Mitchell in *Woman's Estate*, Ann Oakley in *Woman's Work*, and Sheila Rowbotham in *Woman's Consciousness, Man's World*, were among those who argued that women's labor in the home (which included both household chores and child-care) went largely unrecognized and uncompensated, even though this labor comprised part of the gross national product (GNP) and ensured that paid laborers under capitalism were able to reproduce themselves.[47] Moreover, as Engels had opined, the saddling of women with unpaid and unrecognized labor in the home simultaneously ensured their ongoing state of dependency and subordination. Consequently, Marxist feminists advocated attempts to call social attention to the need to compensate women's work in the home. These efforts are certainly interesting to note even though little came of them. Why? One obvious reason is that, from the inception of Reaganism in the 1980s through the present, social emphasis has shifted to how to cut budgets rather than expanding them: in this context, though, who was to pay wages for housework? If the state, the question immediately arises as to whose taxes would have to be tapped and for how much; if male husbands or partners, how would that actually work? The practical complexities of such a plan may have made it unlikely that it would come to fruition under conditions where capitalism itself remained in place.

A second issue that interested Marxists feminists was comparable worth. Comparable worth was a policy aimed at forcing companies to re-evaluate the value they attached to a wide range of job categories. According to sociologist Ronnie Steinberg, whose work was influential in promoting this idea, job categories in which women predominate tend to be paid less than job categories in which men predominate even if one can argue that the two are approximately equal in social value.[48] Thus a company that employed men as truck drivers might pay them more than the administrative assistants in the firm who tended to be women. Comparable worth suggested that the value to the firm of both jobs needed to be re-evaluated in such a way that "women's work" was more generously and equally rewarded. Moreover if this were to happen across the economy, as Marxist feminists familiar with analyses like Steinberg's argued, the economically disadvantaged position in which women as a group found themselves might collectively improve.

Marxist feminist approaches therefore could be said to draw theoretical inspiration from Engels' analysis in *The Origins of the Family*.[49] Like Engels, this perspective did not overlook class-based differences between women but, instead, accorded them a primary place. Unless the relationship between working women's economic stresses and their gender-based subordination was recognized (a relationship that was obviously different for upper-class women), it would be impossible for women to break away from the dual discriminations they experienced. On the other hand, perhaps because Marxist feminist analyses can be traced back in part to Engels, some of these analyses can be criticized for reductionism of exactly the opposite kind that characterized radical feminist analyses. For some Marxist feminists tended to presume that gender subordination could be reduced to a function of class; one senses that were capitalism to be overcome (and women better compensated economically for their labor outside and inside the workplace), the problem of sexism would wither away. As with radical feminist thought, though, such a conclusion seems far too simplistic, failing to place several forms of discrimination in a more balanced and intellectually precise relationship with one another. However, to the extent that they were distinguishable from Marxist feminists, socialist feminists sought, in effect, to avoid this problem of reductionism – that is, of according causal priority to one factor to explain a phenomenon (like capitalism or patriarchy) that seems on closer examination to have multiple roots.

4 Socialist feminism

Whereas Marxist feminism tended to use class to explain women's subordination, socialist feminists were notable for their commitment to understanding how capitalist class oppression and gender-based subordination were equally significant in their inter-relationship with one another. As indicated by the title of one well-known socialist feminist text edited by Zillah Eisenstein, *Capitalist Patriarchy and the Case for Socialist Feminism*, the two systems – capitalism and patriarchy – often functioned as though one.[50] Consequently, one goal of socialist feminism was to merge the most important insights of radical feminist and Marxist feminist theories.

This meant that socialist feminists were committed to the development of historically specific, more than universalistic, analyses. For example, in her essay "Developing a Theory of Capitalist Patriarchy," Eisenstein presented the following diagrammatic grid of "capitalist patriarchy" aimed at showing how both systems interacted in women's day-to-day life experiences (see table 2.1 below). On the vertical axis of this grid, Eisenstein laid out six different class positions in which women found themselves from wealthy/not working, working/professional, and working/nonprofessional through housewives, welfare recipients, and unemployed.

Along the horizontal axis of this diagram are five specifically gender-related aspects of women's situation: reproduction, child-rearing, maintenance of home, sexuality, and consumption. The utility of this diagram is that it allows us to develop hypothetical examples, in a number of concrete areas, of how women are likely to differ according to their differing class positions within what Eisenstein dubs "capitalist patriarchies."

Examples suggested by this grid are easily elaborated. On the one hand, a poor and unemployed woman is obviously of the same gender as an independently wealthy woman. Indeed, through the gender commonality they share, both are potentially affected by any restrictions that may develop on women's rights to reproductive freedom. On the other hand, class differences greatly affect this seeming commonality so that the more well-to-do woman is likely to enjoy more reproductive freedom in practice than the poorer woman even under restricted conditions (for example, if

Table 2.1

	Reproduction	Child-rearing	Maintenance of home	Sexuality	Consumption
Unemployed women					
Welfare					
Houseworkers (housewives)					
Working women outside of home: nonprofessional					
Working women outside of home: professional					
Wealthy women who do not work (even in own home)					

Source: Zillah Eisenstein (ed.), *Capitalist Patriarchy and the Case for Socialist Feminism*, New York: Monthly Review Press, 1978, p. 33.

the *Roe* v. *Wade* Supreme Court decision that legalized abortion in the US in 1973, were to be overturned). Actually, even *with Roe* v. *Wade* in place since the 1970s, poor women have encountered difficulties in receiving federal funding for abortion should they need it. A host of other examples of class-related differences in daily life experiences can be cited. Clearly, a poor or working-class woman cannot outsource housework duties, as can the upper-class woman who has the option to employ a nanny and/or cleaning lady. She may have less time to enjoy her intimate relationships or, should she encounter battering or sexual harassment, may not be able to exit from the situation because of financial dependency.

This characteristic of merging gender-based and class-based analyses has also influenced the issues with which socialist feminists have tended to be concerned. For example, prostitution or "sex work" would be difficult to understand unless class and gender discrimination were accorded co-equal theoretical importance. Clearly this issue encompasses class-based problems of the kind that preoccupied Marxist feminists: ethnographic research leaves little doubt that most women who become involved with sex work do so because of financial necessity rather than out of academic curiosity and genuine choice.[51] Simultaneously the very fact of prostitution's existence, and the disproportionate numbers of women involved with sex work over time, attest to the verity of radical feminist beliefs that controls exerted over women's bodies are central to gender-based discrimination and power.

While Marxist feminism and socialist feminism therefore each high-lighted class differences between women, albeit in different ways, they too have been criticized for not being inclusive enough. While Marxist and socialist feminists stressed the class-based differences liberal and radical feminist theories had overlooked, writer Bell Hooks began in the 1980s to examine even these difference-oriented feminisms' relative quiescence when it came to questions of race.

5   Black feminist thought

Bell Hooks, Michelle Wallace, and Patricia Hill Collins are certainly not household names.[52] Yet, to understand how gender has been defined and eventually refined through the recent history of the feminist movement – especially in the second-wave US context – these writers' contributions must be discussed because of the significant moral and intellectual influence they have exerted. Here, I start by delineating how Hooks' writings were important in the development of contemporary feminisms before moving to sociologist Patricia Hill Collins' perspectives as expressed in her now well-known work of sociology, *Black Feminist Thought*.

A recurring theme in Bell Hooks' early writings, particularly in her books *Ain't I a Woman* and *Feminist Theory from Margin to Center*, was that black women had been rendered invisible throughout US history in general and feminist history in particular. On the one hand, Hooks contended that historians usually emphasized, among the range of dread-ful problems that plagued African American families under slavery, the "emasculation" of black men that resulted from their inability to be breadwinners for their families. Hooks' point was that the notion of emasculation presumed that the normal place of black men was in families where another dominance/subordination relationship was al-ready taken for granted – that is, controls that black men could legitim-ately exert over black women within traditionally, or patriarchally, organized nuclear families.

On the other hand, the scarce attention paid black women in feminist writings from the 1970s onward – from liberal and radical feminist treatises through socialist feminist writings including even Eisenstein's class dif-ference-oriented writings, as discussed above – created an intellectual lacunae.[53] Most branches of feminist thought appeared unaware that issues of racial differences between women – and the problems that many women of color encountered along with gender- and class-based biases – were of concern. Yet, as Hooks pointed out, racism had always been there.

For instance, the famed founding figures of first-wave American feminism, including Elizabeth Cady Stanton and Susan B. Anthony, failed to address – however assertive they were in other areas – the invisibility of black women when it came to voting rights.[54] In fact, some early feminists opposed extending suffrage to black men, choosing instead to exploit racist arguments and pander to the white supremacist ideology of anti-suffragists as a strategy of expediency.[55] Although the suffragettes voiced some concern about the situation of black women in particular and blacks in general, blacks were not part of their political calculus.[56] As historian Rosalind Rosenberg has stated: "Race proved the one insurmountable obstacle in the suffrage campaign."[57] Nor did the situation appear to improve later on. Hooks surveyed a number of writings of later feminists – from the liberal feminist work of Betty Friedan to, again, the socialist feminist work of Zillah Eisenstein – only to find that systematic consideration of how racial differences among women affected feminist theory had not appeared.[58] Thus, whereas writings in American history left out black women (by prioritizing problems faced by black men), American feminist writings left out race altogether (by prioritizing problems faced by white women): the end result in both literatures was that black women remained invisible. In this regard, Hooks' analysis offers another example of reductionism: perspectives that reduced understanding of black women's circumstances to a sole matter of either race or gender failed to consider the multi-dimensional complexity of all women's experiences.[59]

Hooks' work therefore aimed (a) to show past invisibility and (b) to stress the importance of simultaneously taking gender, class, and race into account in future analyses that seek to understand the complex forms of discrimination faced by black women and other women of color. In *Black Feminist Thought*, Patricia Hill Collins went further to suggest that perspectives committed to including all three kinds of discriminations in their analyses – that is not only gender and class but race as well – comprised their own distinctive theoretical orientation.

In making her case for the importance of black feminist thought, Collins drew on standpoint theory.[60] Standpoint theories argue that social discriminations are best understood from the viewpoint of a person who is directly, and experientially, affected. For example, the capitalist system is obviously bound to look different depending on whether one views it from the position of a worker or a capitalist; in this sense, Marxist thought can be said to exemplify a standpoint theory. Moreover such theories contend that an oppressed party's standpoint is more inclusive than that of an oppressor. In the Marxist tradition, Hegel's master/slave dialectic involved the assertion that slaves understood both their own situations and, by dint of their forced situation, how the master saw the world as well.[61] In other words, the oppressed party was forced to take the role of the other as well as her/his own in order to survive. In *Money, Sex, and Power* socialist feminist Nancy Hartsock applied standpoint theory to class and gender-based situations.[62] According to Hartsock, understanding the standpoint of women who experienced class and gender subordination was necessary to undermine the entwined character of capitalism and patriarchy. Otherwise, capitalism would be only partially uprooted.

In *Black Feminist Thought*, Collins extends such analyses to assert that the situation of women of color, who often encounter gender, class, and racial biases simultaneously, offers the deepest standpoint from which to build an inclusive feminist theory.[63] According to Collins, because a working-class woman of color experiences discrimination based on gender, race, and class, her situation cannot be reduced to a single causal factor. Other feminists and social theorists may argue with Collins' own viewpoint. One possible criticism is to wonder where this line of thinking ends: by the logic of standpoint theory, would the perspective of a poor woman of color who was lesbian offer the deepest and most legitimate standpoint? What if that person was also disabled, and then what about distinctions of class among those who are disabled? But, regardless of whether such a potentially absurd infinite regress suggests one problem with Collins' perspective, and that of standpoint theory generally, writings on black feminism from Hooks to Collins have played a central role in the unfolding of contemporary feminisms. As a result, by 2005, it is far less likely that women's (or men's) problems will be viewed or studied in one-dimensional terms. Indeed, to exemplify the influence of black feminist thought on the development of perspectives that consider gender, race, and class discriminations simultaneously, we turn to the work of yet another sociologist who has incorporated these three dimensions. In this case, though, she has done so in an empirical rather than theoretically based piece of scholarship.

Refining Gender: from Theory to Practice

An excellent illustration of the movement of gender from liberal and radical feminist orientations to perspectives that incorporated race, class, and gender into their analyses can be found in sociologist Judith Rollins' interesting study *Between Women: Domestics and Their Employers*.[64] For her doctoral dissertation, Rollins conducted a participant observation study with women who worked as domestics for other women. This allowed Rollins to investigate both commonalities among women and differences between them based on class and race positions. All the domestic employees that Rollins interviewed were black working-class women and all the employers were white middle- or upper-middle-class women.

Rollins' findings confirmed that differences between women were as significant as the liberal and radical feminist tendency to stress commonalities also worthy of note. On the level of commonalities, gender has meant that women much more than men have historically been assigned (and later associated with) domestic work, including both housework and child-care. But Rollins' study also emphasized that a sign of status for middle- and upper-class white women has often been the class-based ability to hire other women – usually much poorer women and often women of color – to do socially devalued household work for them. Here, a power relationship "between women" arises wherein the party with relative power is the white middle-class employer and the party who is relatively powerless is the working-class black woman.

Moreover, domestic work can be distinguished from regular paid labor in at least three ways. One is that domestic labor occurs in what seems like a pre-capitalist rather than capitalist setting, often entirely unregulated by the state and bestowing few if any benefits on workers. Second, domestic work usually takes place between women, thereafter becoming an unusually intimate and gendered one-on-one relationship in and of itself. Finally, domestic labor occurs in the private sphere of a home rather than in a large public space where many workers can observe dynamics between boss and bossed that may lead to collective politicization. This situation of privatization may make it circumstantially difficult for domestic employees to organize into labor unions of their own.

According to Rollins, what is also distinctive about this particular power relationship is that employers often took what she calls a "maternalistic" (rather than paternalistic) attitude toward their domestic employees. Her study concluded that white middle-class employers often appeared to be treating their employees in apparently nurturing ways that reflected their own gendered backgrounds. For instance, it was common to find employers referring to their employees by nicknames, and attempting to be nice by offering them old clothing and hand-me-downs. Nevertheless, Rollins showed how "rituals of subordination" subtly came into play; domestics often experienced their boss's overtures as inappropriate and demeaning.[65] For instance, employers would sometimes turn off the heat and lights and lock the doors even though the domestics remained in the home; these omissions vividly illustrated what Hooks meant by black women experiencing invisibility. Other rituals of subordination involved acts of linguistic deference such as, perhaps, calling one's employee "girl" or by that person's first name whether or not a person felt comfortable with her employer doing so. Rollins also documented acts of spatial-based deference, such as communicating to a domestic worker that she was more welcome in the kitchen and bathrooms of a home than in its main living areas.

Between Women exemplifies standpoint theory in one interesting respect. Because their jobs entailed pleasing their female bosses, Rollins found that domestic employees perceived both their own situations and that of their employers in terms of overlapping gender, racial, and class-based discriminations. Interestingly, Rollins also emphasized that employees developed a particular form of "ressentiment" that they did not internalize. Hypothetically, one might predict that the employers' unwittingly demeaning actions and statements might have come to make employees feel badly about themselves. According to Rollins, though, many women who worked as domestics knew that the discrimination they experienced was not of their own making. Possessed of confidence that Rollins suggests may have come from a firm sense of belonging to their neighborhoods and churches, women working as domestics felt mistreatment they encountered was not their fault but their employers'.

Other more recent writings have continued to explore gender, race, and class interrelationships as they affect distinctively "women's work." In particular, a number of journalists and scholars are currently examining differences between women in the context of immigration. One case in point is an essay by Arlie Russell Hochschild in *Global Woman: Nannies, Maids and Sex Workers in the New Economy*. Hochschild argues that women from poorer countries are often compelled, for economic reasons, to import "love and care" to children they care for in richer places so as to support their own children left at home.[66] Another important sociological study in this area was done by Pierrette Hondagneu-Sotelo in *Domestica: Immigrant Workers Cleaning and Caring in the Shadows of Influence*. Hondagneu-Sotelo looked at the role played by Mexican and Central American (particularly Salvadoran and Guatemalan) immigrant women who work as housekeepers and nannies in the Los Angeles economy.[67] In this respect like Rollins, Hondagneu-Sotelo also studied a relationship that occurs primarily between women.

As we conclude this chapter on gender, it is clear that the topic itself can no longer be conceived narrowly as it unfolded in scope from the 1970s to the present. We have shown different ways of defining gender, emphasizing how critiques of reductionism have made it virtually impossible to ignore the relationship between gender and other forms of discrimination such as ones based on class and race. But what about definitions of race – did these, too, need to be refined as anti-racist theorists and activists encountered some of the very gender-based insights that have been recounted in this chapter?

CHAPTER THREE

Complicating Race: a Multi-Dimensional Approach

Complexifying? As we would sometimes comment to students of "Gender, Race, and Class" classes at Barnard/Columbia or Fordham, the multi-dimensional character of this subject matter suggests a need for nuanced concepts and refined terminology. In the previous chapter, this was exemplified by defining gender to encompass both the commonalities among women that liberal and radical feminists theorized and the differences that Marxist, socialist, and black feminists (among a range of activists, writers, and scholars who developed this perspective) aptly underscored. Certainly, the unfolding of feminisms from the 1970s through the present makes clear that simplistic approaches are inadequate. Correspondingly, the present chapter is organized in two sections to show, first, varied ways that "race" itself has been defined and, secondly, the intellectual importance of according this term the complexity it deserves. This is illustrated in the latter half of the chapter where we look at how academic studies that acknowledge discriminations based on race, but do not consider ones based on gender and class, may be limited in their ability to represent the social world's actual multi-dimensionality.

At the outset, then, it seems sensible to note that some contemporary theorists refer to race and others to "race." Why? While sociological approaches have differentiated between sex and gender (see chapter 2), the former alluding to biological distinctions and the latter to social/cultural constructions, an analogous distinction has not so conventionally been made regarding "race" as opposed to race. Yet, theorists of "race" sometimes use quotation marks to emphasize, as sociologists have done in the area of gender, the deeply constructed character of the term.[1] Is there such a thing as "race" in and of itself? Recall from chapter 2 that most people initially ask "Is it a boy or a girl?" when they learn, from a friend or relative, that a baby has just been born. Yet it is easy to imagine an alternative world where a child's sex – sex being, as Judith Butler has argued, itself a culturally conditioned term – was deemed less important than inquiring about, say, that child's weight or health.[2] Analogously, can't we envision a world where race, as we now use the word, had also become a transcended category, indeed, passé? Cornel West entitled his bestselling 1993 book *Race Matters*[3] and, in our present world, it does: soon to be presented is a definition that likely approximates the way in which West intended the term. But perhaps the goal of people concerned about gender and racial discrimination should be for "sex" and "race" to become obsolete categories, and for biases built upon them to have withered away (even if this means that academics who teach these subjects, and writers who write about them, would have to find alternative areas of study). Thus, some critics' insistence on referring to "race" reflects a determined intellectual bent not only toward emphasizing the constructed but also the historically contingent character of the word. It has been effectively argued that race can only be understood as a dynamic and flexible sociohistorical construct and that notions of race as an ideological construct or "objective condition" are flawed.[4] Hence, the meaning and significance of race are continuously evolving over time and across geographic space.

In the sense West intended, race still matters if we define it in terms of physiological distinctions of skin color or the phrenology it is often used to connote. The range of scholars and disciplines that use the term to denote physiological difference is wide, from polygenists to criminologists to sociobiologists to anthropologists to psychoanalysts to philosophers to historians.[5] Such physiologically based usages could, in theory, have quite neutral meanings; one can imagine some word (whether "race" or a substitute linguistic connotation) persisting indefinitely to descriptively connote differences in the color of people's skins. On the other hand, race has been regularly used in socially constructed processes of racialization that construct biases and differences on the basis of skin color. For many centuries the Western world has accorded superiority to lighter skin types and relative inferiority to darker skin types, as biologically based shades of distinction came to reflect cultural and social prejudices. Similarly, in South Africa and Brazil the emergence of a strict white/black dialectic established patterns of race-based discrimination that were, as in the United States, ultimately legally encoded.[6] Just as Simone de Beauvoir bemoaned the spurious persistence of a "second sex," so racialization has too often, in recent history, set up hierarchies between skin types, most notably Caucasian, and "others."[7]

But this depiction is more complicated still since not every definitional perspective has concurred in equating race only with skin color. In this chapter, we will be defining race in four ways, following but also elaborating on the range of defining perspectives used by Michael Omi and Howard Winant in the theoretical sections of their frequently cited work *Racial Formation in the United States.*[8] Omi and Winant define race through four "paradigms" that are, respectively, ethnicity-based, class-based, nation-based, and, last but not least, one based upon viewing race as an autonomous factor in and of itself. In this final perspective, drawing on the conceptual vocabulary introduced in chapter 1, Omi and Winant try to remedy the problems of reductionism with a paradigm that cannot be "reduced" to anything other than itself.

After detailing each of these paradigms, and providing more recent analyses and illustrations in relation to them, the second part of this chapter turns to whether and how the race-based paradigm becomes more complex – as did the gender-based paradigm elaborated in chapter 2 – when other social factors are incorporated and co-considered. Omi and Winant's paradigms hardly accounted for the place of gender – if we explore this omission through literary and popular cultural examples, does it turn out to be significant? Omi and Winant did take class into account in various ways, but does the race/class debate to which they refer continue to wage through the 1980s and 1990s? Has any progress been made, theoretically or in practice, beyond that debate?

The Ethnicity Paradigm

Students are sometimes unsure about how to define race as opposed to ethnicity – how are they related, and how are they different? Again, the term "race" has conventionally denoted physiognomy. By contrast, ethnicity is usually defined more broadly such that race – by a physiological definition – is only one of its components. For instance, in *Race and Racism*, Van Den Berghe notes that definitions of race have varied greatly from the biological category of skin color to shared cultural characteristics (for example, the French race) to its use as a synonym for species (as in the human race). Ethnicity, on the other hand, is usually defined in terms of cultural criteria – common language, social customs, national and political identification, religion, group processes. It is commonly used to denote characteristics that give groups a sense of durable connection with, and loyalty to, one another; from this, a sense of identity, and specifically an ethnic identity, can emerge over time.[9] Accordingly common customs and cultural heritage, including religion and language, are components of ethnicity as are factors of region (and sometimes nationality) and race (that is, skin color).

Tensions between race, ethnicity, and nationality are often heightened in urbanized regions. For example, the racial and ethnic diversity of New York City's inhabitants has shaped its character. Prior to the Immigration Act of 1965, immigrants of European ancestry flooded the metropolis, recreating the cultural and social texture of their native homelands through language, traditions, religion, customs, and foods. In the latter half of the twentieth century, immigrants from South America, Central America, Asia, Africa, Europe, and the Caribbean spread out across the city creating new ethnic communities and making New York one of the most diverse cities in the nation. Since 1990, no single racial or ethnic group has constituted a majority of the city's residents.[10] Many New Yorkers continue to reside in ethnic enclaves marked by social and cultural homogeneity. Consequently, one might say that Russian Americans who live near one another in Brighton Beach, Brooklyn, in New York, one of the most enduring ethnic enclaves, share a sense of ethnic identity insofar as they reside in the same neighborhood, speak the same Russian dialect in many cases, and have perhaps immigrated to the United States under similar conditions; in addition, they may share the same religion and frequently eat similar foods.

Yet, the borough of Brooklyn houses numerous ethnic groups with varied racial identities, including West Indians, Puerto Ricans, and Brazilians. The extent to which ethnicity differs from race (as defined by skin color) is apparent if we consider that within these diverse ethnic groups in Brooklyn, skin colors range from lighter-skinned to darker-skinned, with innumerable variations in between. In her classic study of West Indians, *Black Identities*, Mary C. Waters notes that many "immigrants enter the United States with experience of a different racial and ethnic categorization system – one that recognizes a variety of categories between black and white."[11] And Anthony Marx describes a similar distinction for Brazilians who immigrate from a country where, he writes, "the state embraced a cultural focus on 'color more than 'race,' thereby reinforcing the salience of a wide array of physical differences rather than potentially antagonistic larger groupings."[12] People who live in New York City and who are originally from Puerto Rico may feel that they share the same ethnicity because (as in the example of Russian Americans) they eat similar foods, live in the same vicinity, migrated under similar circumstances, and identify strongly with cultural customs. Moreover, some of these customs may originate in the home country; some may have developed here (as part of second generation immigration), or both. Simultaneously, as Clara Rodriguez has noted, race in the sense of skin color may again vary within these groups.[13] *The Idea of Race in Latin America, 1870–1940* examines the process through which European-based scientific racism emerged as the dominant ideology despite the racial heterogeneity of the Latino population.[14] Similarly, in China and Japan, the formation of racial identity based upon the discourse of blood affinity enables majority communities to distinguish themselves from minority communities in the absence of clear distinctions between race and ethnicity.[15] Thus, ethnic groups may frequently be racially heterogeneous and the persistence of discrimination across nations based upon racial categories may impede possibilities of political solidarity based solely on the latter.[16]

To trace the emergence of ethnicity-based theories of race in the US context, Omi and Winant identify three historical stages of its development. The first was from the 1920s to 1930s, and involved an explicit challenge to social Darwinism, Spencer, and eugenics that took racial inferiority to be "natural" based on the alleged superiority of whites (other skin colors were seen as inferior), and assumed race to be the single determinant of character traits and genetic predispositions. Omi and Winant date a second stage as stretching from the 1930s to 1965 when race (like gender) was viewed through the lens of progressivism. At this point, the social construction of race was based on two basic concepts: assimilationism (introduced by Robert E. Parks and the "Chicago school" of sociology) which held that, over time, minority groups would slowly accept and be accepted into the majority culture; and cultural pluralism (introduced by Horace Kelley) which held that some ethnic group identity would remain even after assimilation. Finally, the third period these authors identified started after 1965, when race and ethnicity became the foci of a neo-conservative backlash against anti-discrimination policies.[17]

As with different feminisms, ethnicity-based theories of race also contributed to the forging of reductionistic habits of thought. One important criticism of the ethnicity paradigm is that, as Omi and Winant note, it lends itself easily to the notion that minority groups needed only to "pull themselves up by their bootstraps" in order to advance. For one thing, the problem with this notion is that it assumes equivalent historical and social circumstance across ethnic groups. By extension, if a group works hard enough – that is, its members are sufficiently industrious and follow the American dream – it presumes they will succeed in the socially fluid, welcoming melting pot that is the United States. However, in both historical and theoretical terms, this has not always been the case. Contradicting such sanguine assertions are two important texts that give the lie to the notion of ethnic and racial homogeneity in both theoretical and empirical terms.

For instance, Stephen Thernstrom's well-known *The Other Bostonians* showed that, between 1890 and 1930, the class and occupational position of blacks in Boston failed to improve substantially over three generations. By contrast, Irish and other European immigrants living in Boston during the same period did experience inter-generational improvements, moving from manual labor jobs into a relatively greater proportion of white-collar positions. In 1880, 11 percent of first-generation and 25 percent of second-generation Irish immigrants had white-collar jobs compared to 9 percent of first-generation and 12 percent of second-generation black Southern migrants. By 1890, 14 percent of first-generation and 32 percent of second-generation Irish immigrants, and 11 percent of first-generation and 17 percent of second-generation black Southern migrants had white-collar jobs. Yet, third-generation blacks – those born in the North to Northern-born fathers – made no gains between 1880 and 1890; the same proportion, 17 percent, held white-collars jobs.

More striking yet are census data that show the percentage of first-generation immigrants in white-collar and skilled jobs, 24 percent and 30 percent respectively, as being more than double that of blacks, 11 percent and 12 percent respectively, by 1930. Black Bostonians made few advances between 1890 and 1940; in 1890, 56 percent were unskilled laborers; in 1940, five decades later, 53 percent remained unskilled laborers. Citing the work of Elizabeth Pleck, Thernstrom notes that the lack of mobility was not the result of single-parent households, as is generally assumed; in 1880 husband and wife were present in 82 percent of black households, with only 16 percent being "female-headed." Instead, as he writes, "there were definite rigidities in the occupational structure, a series of barriers that impeded mobility and perpetuated inequality."[18]

Based on more contemporary evidence, Stephen Steinberg's *The Ethnic Myth* makes a similar argument from a sociological perspective. Steinberg, too, shows that any notion that holds that all ethnicities have been treated equally in the American context fails to take into account the distinctive legacies of racism. Again, empirical evidence is presented that attests to greater difficulties that minorities have experienced. For instance, the history of slavery figures into the backgrounds of African Americans in a way that has no parallel for other groups in American history.[19] And, as both Thernstrom and Steinberg demonstrate, rather than vanishing, deeply seated biases have had ongoing and long-lasting effects.

Another way of making the same point is to note how, until recently, ethnic and racial groups in the United States have been referred to unequally in common discourse. People often refer to immigrant ethnic groups, say, as Italians, Irish, Russians, Korean, Chinese, Mexicans, or Puerto Ricans. In so doing, they use the name of the country or place from which they emigrated. Yet, there is no analogous use of ethnicity when people speak of "blacks" regardless of whether they are referring to West Indians, Jamaicans, Haitians (that is, Afro-Caribbeans) or to people who may be Nigerians, Ethiopians, or African Americans.[20] Consequently, as Omi and Winant suggest, racial prejudices in and of themselves may result in erasure of classificatory ethnic distinctions.[21]

What emerges, then, is that to view race as a component of ethnicity lessens the historical specificity of the former as this has been the occasion for constructing, and enacting, extreme biases over time. Moreover, returning to chapter 1's conceptual vocabulary, such a subordinating of race under the aegis of the ethnicity paradigm is reductionistic. In other words, race becomes seen too one-dimensionally as a function of ethnicity (as though the two were equivalent), thereby obscuring the independent strength of racism as an explanatory factor on its own.

The Class-Based Paradigm

Of course, ethnicity is not the only paradigm within which race has been defined. Race has also been understood in relation to a second paradigm identified by Omi and Winant, namely, class-based perspectives. Here, as they write, "class theories" of race "principally explain race by reference to economic processes, understood in the standard sense of the creation and use of material resources."[22] More specifically, within this paradigm, three types of class-based explanations can be identified: (a) a market relations approach; (b) a class conflict theory; and (c) stratification theory.

Market-based approaches take as given the idea that racism is an impediment to the free workings of the market system (or, as Omi and Winant describe this, "race appears as an anomaly in the equilibrium-oriented theoretical system – an obstacle to market processes"[23]). For academics or writers with this orientation, a prime exponent was conservative economist Milton Friedman, who argues that market equilibrium can be "disrupted" by three factors: racism (which, in this perspective, is seen as an "irrational prejudice"); monopolistic practices that give priority to special interests; and state practices that themselves "disrupt" the workings of the free market system through regulation and over-regulation. What the market approach thereby implies is that, in a perfect world where capitalistic markets are left alone to function as they ought, racism would not exist.[24] But this assertion is flawed in being both circular and, again, reductionistic. Racism, proponents of the theory like Friedman are apt to say, would disappear if capitalist markets were left to work efficiently on their own; at the same time, according to such theorists, racism is one of the factors that impedes the market from working. What, then, brings about racism? Because racism is not recognized as a problem that may well have its own stubborn causes and history, market theorists end up reducing that problem away and fail to explain its origins adequately.

While class conflict approaches are more persuasive in one sense, in another they are the mirror-image opposite of market-based approaches. Whereas market-based approaches see the free market system as potentially leveling the playing field of participants (and thereby capable of reducing or eliminating racism), class conflict approaches see capitalism as incubating racism. Whereas market-based approaches return to laissez-faire markets as the best antidote to skin-based discriminations, class conflict theorists cite at least two reasons for their belief that racism is likely to subsist until/if the time comes when the capitalist system has been overthrown.

One reason is the apparent tendency of the capitalism system to perpetuate racism through a divide-and-conquer mentality. Another way of putting this is that racism is functional to capitalism. The argument goes as follows: if people who work for wages resent one another on the basis of skin color or ethnic affiliation, then they are less likely to realize and act upon their common class interests as workers. This benefits the capitalist system by diminishing the possibilities of successful socialist or union organizing, and by distracting attention from collectively experienced economic grievances. Indeed, American labor history is replete with examples, older and more recent, of racial and ethnic prejudices dividing the workforce against itself. In the 1880s, Chinese workers were used as strike-breakers; this caused widespread resentment of the Chinese, a bias that was evidenced in the writings of American Federation of Labor President Samuel Gompers.[25] Historian Herbert Guttman has documented waves of immigration that create feelings of resentment on the part of older ethnic and racial groups toward the newer arrivals.[26] Within contemporary popular culture, a scene from Spike Lee's film *Do the Right Thing* also gives a sense of how deeply racial and ethnic prejudices run in working people's everyday consciousness. In this scene, a group of people are shown, each of whom is saying something negative about the next person in the circle they form: an Italian American is shown expressing prejudices against people who are black; a person who is black is shown saying he dislikes Koreans; a Korean is shown saying she dislikes the Jews; and so on. Such commonly aired sentiments about racially and ethnically based biases tend to obfuscate similarities such as economic hardships that may serve to unify people.

Segmentation theories comprise a second interpretation of how racial classifications can be functional for the capitalist system.[27] Here, emphasis is placed not so much on the interests of capital in maintaining racism but on the segmentation and "split labor" that occurs among workers themselves. Looking back at American labor history again reveals ongoing divisions between skilled and unskilled workers; workers in the former category have often tried to protect themselves, maintaining their own skill-based superiority, over workers in the latter. Here, racial categories may overlap with class-based ones insofar as unskilled workers may be of the same race or ethnicity that comes to be disliked by older skilled workers who may themselves be of the same race and ethnicity.[28] In this way, race/ethnicity and class-segmented position are occluded in such a way that people express resentments about the former that may have been stirred by resentments originating from capitalist dynamics (say, for example, people have experienced poor workplace conditions, low pay, or dismissals). Whereas training workers overall and providing good job security and benefits for workers as a whole is arguably the solution to the problem of occupational segmentation in the capitalist system, people come, through their biases, to blame particular racial/ ethnic groups for their problems. Again, then, racism emerges as an essential factor in the capitalist system's long-term survival.

The third and last class-based approach to defining race is stratification theory. For the purposes of this chapter, we will treat the writings of William Julius Wilson as the foremost examples of stratification approaches to race. Wilson, a sociologist, has consistently argued that, following the civil rights era of the 1960s and 1970s, class has become more important than race for understanding the situation of racial minorities – especially the situation of African Americans – in the United States. According to Wilson, an important feature of the post-civil rights era has been the development of a black middle class. But, unlike earlier decades in American history when the black middle class lived side by side with poorer and working-class blacks, blacks with the financial wherewithal have deserted blighted inner city neighborhoods in favor of suburban or wealthier urban minority enclaves.[29] In the process, an increasingly impoverished black "underclass" was created that lacked a thriving inner city infrastructure that includes business and job opportunities, transportation, and good education to sustain it. Hence, Wilson argues that class became more important than race in determining the life-chances of African Americans generally but, in particular, the opportunities (or lack thereof) available to poorer members of the group who were left behind. The influential character of Wilson's ideas and writings – as espoused in *The Declining Significance of Race* (first published in 1978), *The Truly Disadvantaged* (1987), and *When Work Disappears* (1996) – contributed to an ongoing race/class debate in social scientific circles (explained in detail below).[30] Most germane for the moment, though, is to note that this race/class debate suggested that, without the leveling of economic inequalities in American society, it was impossible to define adequately the effects of racism. But, once again, this perspective seems reductionistic. Just as market-based approaches suggest that racism would disappear if impediments to the market were removed, class conflict approaches suggest that prejudices would wither away if capitalism were overturned. Is this borne out by empirical analysis? Take, for example, the history of Communist societies, which sought to reduce class-based inequalities (even if they failed at eliminating them entirely). Nonetheless, in a Communist country like the former Yugoslavia, ethnic and racially based resentments did not simply disappear but resurfaced in disputes between Bosnian Serbs and Croatians (this dispute also involving anti-Muslim religious sentiments). Again, racial biases do not seem explicable in terms of other factors, whether ethnicity (as the term is broadly used in the ethnicity paradigm) or class.

Nation-Based Theories

A third form of explaining race explored by Omi and Winant has to do with nation. Nation-based theories take geography, or place, as their primary means of explaining the development and persistence of racially biased sentiments. Again, as in class-based theories, Omi and Winant identify a varied group of perspectives that fit under this analytic umbrella: (a) Pan-Africanism; (b) cultural nationalism; (c) the "national question," as it was called through Marxist debates in the US; and (d) internal colonialism.

Pan-Africanism refers to efforts to "link the specific forms of oppression which blacks face in various societies with the colonialist exploitation and underdevelopment of Africa."[31] The spatially based argument presented in this first type of nation-based theory is that imperialistic countries, through slavery, forced Africans to be separated from each other in colonies all over the world. Moreover, if this is the cause of racism, then the "solution" to this social ill is to reunify people who have been coercively separated. Thus, as Omi and Winant recount, one form of Pan-Africanism took shape through a series of conferences, organized by W. E. B. DuBois in Europe and the United States between 1900 and 1945 that sought to decolonize Africa. A second form of Pan-Africanism revolved around Marcus Garvey who, especially in the 1920s, organized large numbers of followers to push for the "redemption" of Africa. The Universal Negro Improvement Association (UNIA) sought to unite blacks around the world "to overcome the racial oppression which had sustained colonialism."[32]

The influence of Pan-Africanism was not limited to the early decades of the twentieth century, and re-emerged in the 1970s. Particularly notable was the association of Malcolm X with Pan-Africanism after he left the Nation of Islam in 1964 and formed the Organization of African-American Unity; Stokely Carmichael was another well-known black power activist of the 1960s who, after 1967, became involved with Pan-Africanism.[33] The movements' effect overall was to focus attention both on spatial explanations of racism and on the use of geographic separation to sustain racism's power.

Cultural nationalism had a slightly different orientation. Whereas Pan-Africanism looked to connections with a homeland continent as a way of overcoming racial subordination, the emphasis of this second nationalistic theory was the common culture and sense of collective identity that racism had created. According to cultural nationalists, a wide range of similarities – from language to art, music, and religion – united people in another form of spatial unity against the prejudices they encountered. A seminal text that developed this argument was Harold Cruse's well-known *The Crisis of the Negro Intellectual* (1967).[34] Cruse contended that blacks in America had developed a common cultural identity in response to oppressive conditions. By extension, "cultural nationalism" could transform these condition by taking over the means of cultural production in the United States. While Cruse's solution to the problem was clearly vague, the importance of his contribution to nationalist debates lay in illustrating a paradoxical by-product of racism: the creation of cultural commonalities, which also provided a seed to racist systems' transcendence.

Note, then, that each nationalist theory was closely connected to a plan of action by which racial subordination could be overcome. So, too, for the third type that Omi and Winant suggest: the "national question" as it made its way into Marxist debates. This theory requires looking back over

American radical history to the chronicles of the American Communist
Party (CPUSA) in the 1930s. In addition to intense labor activism during
that decade, the CPUSA had also become concerned with issues involving
racism (advocating, long before other radical groups, support for inter-
racial marriages). Moreover, debates over Marxist theory that had been
waged in the Soviet context began to be applied in an American one as
well. In this regard, American Communists argued that blacks in the
South formed a separate nation based on race that needed to be recognized
as such. This "Black Nation" thesis held that because discriminated-
against minorities had been brought to the South, they should have a
right to "self-determination" and to secession if so desired. Therefore,
again, the diagnosis of, and proposed solution for, racism were closely
related in this third nation-based theory of race.[35]

Fourth, last, and possibly most easily grasped in contemporary America are nation-based theories that take the notion of internal colonialism as their template. This is an "internal colonialism" very different
from the radical feminist idea developed by Ti-Grace Atkinson (see
chapter 2). This way of understanding racism in the US context goes
back to two well-known works on race written in the 1960s: Stokely
Carmichael's *Black Power* and Robert Blauner's *Racial Oppression in
America*, both of which drew on ideas about black nationalism.[36] In
developing an internal colonialist perspective, these writers argued that
colonies could be forged inside rather than outside a country that
sought to dominate a particular group of people. This process of internal
colonization often involved racial subordination, such that groups were
kept together racially within spatial/geographic territories. More specifically, internal colonies tend to be marked by "cultural dominance and
resistance," "a system of superexploitation," and the "institutionalization of externally based controls" – terms which, taken together, mean
that a given "colony" has been isolated politically and economically
from the rest of a society, thereafter often developing its own "cultural"
means of survival.[37]

Examples in the US context are not difficult to find, going back to the
1960s and 1970s or, for that matter, at present. An inner city ghettoized
area can be envisioned as an "internal colony" insofar as racism has
usually forced residents to be members; usually, they are poor and working class. Simultaneously, ghettoes are often economically marginalized:
jobs are hard to find and low-paying; banks and businesses have left or
abandoned the neighborhood, leaving few jobs behind; housing may well
be deteriorating and left empty; good transportation and schools are
not being provided.[38] Politically, an internal colony can be defined by

officers being extraordinarily visible, the brutal character of law enforcement; clearly, the power of the state is in evidence, making resistance to socioeconomic oppression hard to mount. Nonetheless, as Omi and Winant suggest, cultural protests take place, often in the form of institutions that provide support (churches, for example, and other community organizations) and popular cultural expression (for example, forms of music may develop, like rap, that can give expression to anger felt about emiserated conditions and racism).

In the contemporary setting of his research on Chicago, Loïc Wacquant coined the term "hyper-ghettoization" in the 1990s to denote a transformation he saw occurring over the last decades of the century.[39] Wacquant's theory stressed that, unlike earlier views of ghettoes as places that immigrants left over a period of successive generations (moving into better neighborhoods and raising their economic status), people in "hyper-ghettoized" inner city neighborhoods like the South Side of Chicago were indefinitely marginalized. The hyper-ghetto and its corollary, the prison, emerged as one of four institutions used to oppress African Americans in the United States over the course of three centuries: slavery (1619–1865), Jim Crow (South, 1865–1965), ghetto (North, 1915–68), and hyper-ghetto and prison (1968 onwards). Prisons and the criminal justice system, he argues, systematically exclude blacks from cultural capital, social redistribution, and political participation, in effect perpetuating their "underclass" status.[40] Hyper-ghettoization is thereby reminiscent of the internal colonialist framework insofar as it involves the interaction of racism, economic and political subordination, and territory.

While nation-based theories of internal colonialism continue to be evocative of ongoing racism in the American context, several criticisms can be made of the theory. For one thing, like ethnicity- and class-based theories, nation-based theories also have a tendency toward reductionism. But whereas the former perspectives reduce racism to a function of ethnicity and class, here, racial subordination tends to be reduced to a function of territory. Two logical pitfalls mar the persuasiveness of equating racism and colonialism (whether internal and external). For one thing, as an explanation of racism, nation-based theories overlook the fact that prejudice follows people from place to place: it is not confined to inner city ghettoes or "internal colonies." Thus, for example, Cornel West began *Race Matters* by recounting how, as a habitually fastidious and well-dressed black man, he himself had encountered, in the early 1990s, great difficulties hailing a cab in midtown Manhattan. The setting could not have been more conducive to minimizing racism in, at least, class-based terms: West was wearing a suit and tie; he was standing on the corner of 60th Street and Park Avenue. But whereas cabs stopped for other well-dressed people including a "fellow citizen of European descent," none would pull over for him. Likewise, in 1995, Ellis Cose detailed a set of subtle and not so subtle indignities experienced by middle-class blacks working in office settings where "glass ceilings" are real, however hidden.[41] To explain these manifestations of racism therefore requires a theory that may include spatial (or nation-based) components but is not limited to them. Secondly, and relatedly, the internal colonialism thesis tends to presume that racism will evanesce with colonization. But this has not been historically borne out: post-colonial societies can still be rife with racism that becomes manifested in and out of geographically confined areas.[42]

Thus, while ethnicity-, class-, and nation-based perspectives on race are helpful (and can be utilized within more complex and multi-dimensional theories of race), none are satisfactory in and of themselves. As Omi and Winant go on to argue, the best theory would be one that holds race as, at least to some extent, autonomous – not reducible to a function of anything else, but calling out for its own multi-level explanations. Here, Omi and Winant are worth quoting at length since their definition of race, culled after presenting the strengths and weaknesses of the other perspectives, is one from which the rest of this chapter proceeds. They suggest that: "race is a concept which signifies and symbolizes social conflicts and interests by referring to different types of human bodies." To this, we would add that this usually refers to skin color, or phenotype, since "race," obviously, is not usually used to signify different types of human bodies on the basis of differing genitalia or height or other physiological distinctions. But Winant, in a later text, also asserts that "race" must be placed in a social structural context of "racial formation," defining the latter by tracing how "society is suffused with racial projects, large and small, to which all are subjected ... A vast web of racial projects mediates between the discursive or representational means in which race is identified and signified on the one hand, and the institutional and organizational forms in which it is routined, and standardized on the other."[43] In practice, this theoretical formulation means that "race" and processes of "racial formation" must be investigated in particular and specific social contexts. Most importantly for our purposes, though, is that Omi and Winant end up with a definition of race as a "central axis" of social relations, one that cannot be subsumed analytically when examining actual social experiences. With this in mind, let us return to the complexities of race. Where, more precisely, do class and gender fit in? Race may be autonomous to some extent but it also is constantly interacting with other social axes like class and gender.

In the second half of this chapter, we strive to keep the autonomous character of race in mind while seeking, simultaneously, to push this argument further. So far, it seems clear that race cannot be entirely explained as a function of other social variables (with which it nonetheless interacts) like ethnicity, class, or nation. But, from this, it does not follow that the meaning of racial formation as it affects many people's everyday lives can be grasped without recourse to other social factors. If we go to the opposite extreme, defining race autonomously rather than "complexifying" our understanding of it, problems are again bound to arise. Indeed, the purpose of this chapter's second half is to illustrate where and how attention to other factors, in particular class stratification and gender discriminations, is critical once we turn to actual problems in the social world. For a key challenge is to keep a strongly independent concept of race in analytic tension with an equally strong understanding of class and gender. To attempt this, let us return to the race/class debate that was mentioned, too briefly, above.

"Complexifying" Race through Class

The very persistence of what has been called the race/class debate attests to analytic dissatisfaction with interpretations of the social world that foreground only one or other of these factors. But what, again, is the race/class debate – how did it arise and what are the contentions that have been made on each of its sides? On the class side of the debate, the name of sociologist William Julius Wilson is by far the best known. Throughout Wilson's writings, the argument reappears that, following the civil rights era, class became more determinative of African Americans' life chances in the US than race. As the number of middle-class blacks in America increased, a marginalized underclass was left behind in increasingly deserted and impoverished inner city areas where problems from drugs and crime to broken families became common in the structural context of social abandonment. Jobs, financial resources, and good educational possibilities were not to be found in ghettoized neighborhoods where members of this underclass resided. Moreover, people were far less likely than in earlier generations to be able to escape; their marginalization appeared far more long-lasting, even permanent.

What, then, was to be done? For, arguably, questions of policy are at the heart of the race/class debate: which should one stress, class or race, to ameliorate discriminations that minorities in America continue to face?

According to Wilson, race-based policies spurred by 1960s social move-ments failed significantly to affect the desperate condition faced by the underclass. By race-based policies, he referred primarily to affirmative action programs in hiring and education that Wilson contended had benefited mostly middle-class African Americans. It was the latter, he argued, who had been the prime beneficiaries of programs aimed at redressing, through quotas and other special race-based measures, the legacies of past discrimination.

On the other hand, Wilson believed that class-based policies would bring more meaningful improvements. By class-based policies, he referred to programs aimed at providing universal benefits regardless of race, ethnicity, gender, or other social distinctions. Into this category fell micro- or macro-economic changes in tax policy, for example, or govern-ment-sponsored job creation programs. But universal class-based pro-grams also included measures that would, for instance, provide health insurance to everyone; high quality child-care; economic subsidies to families with children who needed it (as exists in Sweden, Canada, and other countries around the world which have "family policies"); and housing subsidies. For Wilson, the beauty of such universal policies is that they could create what he called a "trickle down" effect. Even if their intention was not directly to improve the life conditions of people who experienced racial discrimination, clearly, upper- and middle-class people would not need (or need to use) these provisions to the same degree as poor, low-income, and working-class people. Thus, an indirect effect – and, as Wilson dubbed it, the "hidden agenda" – of class-based policies was to ameliorate racial discrimination as well. At the same time, of course, Wilson was well aware that racism was a controversial topic in 1980s and 1990s America and remains so to this day. It was not at all clear that voters would elect politicians who promised explicitly to deal with racial biases head on. On the other hand, by attempting to redress racial imbalances through class-based measures, people across the color line might be able to jump on the bandwagon of progressive social change. Not coincidentally, following Bill Clinton's first election in 1992 (and the absence of explicit discussions of racial discrimination in his campaign), Wilson was one of the first advisers the new president called to Washington. It should be pointed out, too, that another benefit of a class-based position is that it suggests one way that "race" could diminish as a social construction in and of itself. While this was not Wilson's stated purpose, universal policies had the benefit of rendering "race" (and therefore racism) unnecessary and eventually, perhaps, even irrelevant.

But not everyone agreed with Wilson's arguments. (Nor, at the time of writing in 2005, soon after President George W. Bush's re-election in late 2004, have universal class policies themselves been embraced: indeed they seem, in the present US context, unfortunately utopian.) The set of arguments made on the race side of the race/class debate differ markedly. Here, a major spokesperson has been Queens College sociologist Stephen Steinberg. In a series of articles published by the democratic socialist journal *New Politics*, Steinberg dissected Wilson's contentions about the inclining significance of class (and, by extension, the increased irrelevance of race). Steinberg's arguments could be broken down into those that were empirically based and those of a more theoretical bent. Overall, from his articles, one could say that the two were connected:

1. Affirmative action was effective, not ineffective. According to Steinberg, empirical evidence about employment patterns in American cities show that little would have altered were it not for race-based affirmative action policies. Citing an employment study of New York City in 1985, Steinberg contended that only 120 out of 200 companies where service sector jobs were created had hired African Americans. Moreover, when one looked closely at where African Americans had been hired, this turned out to be largely in government positions, that is, as a result of affirmative action hires.

2. Use of categories like the "underclass" themselves perpetuate racially based discrimination by emphasizing cultural rather than structural causes, and revealing the depth of distinctly racist thinking. According to Steinberg, Wilson's theorization was a continuation of a very old tendency to stigmatize poor minorities through terms that hid rather than revealed distinctly racial (not only class-based) biases. From the "culture of poverty" terminology initially employed by Oscar Lewis in his 1959 classic *Five Families* through the "tangle of pathology" language of Daniel Moynihan,[44] the concept of a racialized "other" has been deeply embedded in American life. To emphasize class, Steinberg suggested, might call attention away from the depth of racism that needed to be exposed rather than "hidden."[45]

3. The civil rights movement and progress made toward racial justice in America has grown from movements that explicitly stressed, not de-emphasized, racism. Here, Steinberg combined empirical, theoretical, and historically oriented analyses to underscore his conviction that a "hidden agenda" is not likely to work. Only when people refused to accept racial injustices *en masse*, according to Steinberg, had the conditions of minorities in the United States improved.

4. Consequently, racially based affirmative action policies need to be expanded rather than restricted. Steinberg reaches virtually the opposite

conclusion of Wilson: behind ongoing racial discrimination is not too much attention to race-based policies but too little. Rather than doing away with race-based affirmative action, Steinberg calls for its application to inner city areas, including job creation programs and the provision of educational opportunities, where benefits have not yet been felt.

The work of other sociologists provides further confirmation for the race side of the race/class debate. For instance, in *American Apartheid*, Douglas Massey and Nancy Denton build a persuasive case that the most substantial cause of ongoing racial inequality in the United States is residential segregation.[46] Massey and Denton's thesis is that this factor has been relatively overlooked since the 1970s even though they contend that a host of social ills – for example, ongoing educational disparities and economic inequalities based upon race – stem from the sheer persistence of racial segregation. Fascinatingly, they take a persuasive stance in the race/class debate – if not necessarily referring to their analysis as such – by showing that middle-class blacks have not fared that much better in their housing situation.

Going city by city across the United States, *American Apartheid* provides data showing that most blacks and most whites live in census tract areas that are not integrated; little about this has changed, in most cities, over the last 100 years. Massey and Denton show that red-lining policies of banks, and overtly discriminatory policies of realtors, have steered minorities away from certain neighborhoods, effectively enforcing ongoing segregation. Moreover, when one considers middle-class people who are black, there is little change in economic status as we go up the pay scale. Mary Pattillo-McCoy, in a fine ethnographic study of black middle-class families in Chicago, also concludes that while class obviously matters, racial discrimination played an ongoing role in why black middle-class families often encountered economic and social obstacles more severe than those faced by white middle-class families. According to Pattillo-McCoy, problems of the black middle class have tended to be overlooked.[47] From these analyses, it is not much of a stretch to conclude that race (that is, racism) is at least as important as, if not more important than, class in determining African Americans' life chances – this posing a direct challenge to the Wilson position.

But does one have to take an either/or stance in the race/class debate – might it not make more sense to say that both matter? Certainly, following Wilson on the class side, it seems undeniable that class-related problems – among these jobs that are either non-existent or insecure and poorly paid, inadequate or lack of health care and housing; child-care difficulties that poor women regularly face – are a major, if not the major, issue that minority families face. Moreover, one can make a good argument that ignoring class-related problems that regularly create stress for people of all colors has contributed to backlashes among whites against 1960s social movement gains based, more narrowly, on gender and race. For this reason, some critical contemporary legal scholars and other critical race theorists have advocated the inclusion of class as one component of affirmative action programs.[48]

Arguments can be made just as convincingly on the race side of the debate. For, following Steinberg and Massey and Denton, how can it be accidental that poor people are disproportionately members of minority groups? According to Ruth Sidel, in 1993 minority children were two and a half times more likely to live in families whose incomes were below the recorded poverty level; that is more than 46 percent of black children and 41 percent of Hispanic children compared to 14 percent of white children.[49] Again, it seems difficult to deny that explicit (not "hidden") attention to racial dynamics is required if gains – including those made by a black middle class – are ever to occur.

Thus efforts to synthesize both race and class – and in such a way that does not reduce either to the other – seem critical to capture the analytic contributions of both sides in the so-called race/class debate. For Loïc Wacquant, one element of such a synthesis requires recognizing that the debate itself is academic.[50] If we stop to realize that race and class abstract from the necessarily interactive, messily all-caught-up character of actual lived experience, the seemingly dichotomous character of the debate starts to fade away. On the other hand, one could argue, with some cause, that quite apart from academia, real life policy decisions often require emphasizing race *or* class in decision-making. Even if affirmative action did include class, perhaps the added historic discrimination that working-class minorities have experienced makes it necessary to prioritize their experience over that of working-class whites?

Our own view is that efforts need to be made, in theory and practice, to recognize what is distinctive about both racially based and class-based discriminations in order to build political coalitions aimed at improving the conditions of people of all classes and colors. Universal class-based measures – good housing, education, health care, job creation and provision, child-care and supportive family policies – are vital for ensuring the ability of working-class and poor families, across racial and ethnic divisions, to support themselves, to thrive and survive. At the same time, instead of seeing this question in either/or terms, circumstances are likely to arise where historic racial discrimination needs to be prioritized, as in the case of a given union or company that has managed over time to keep blacks or Latino employees out. Perhaps the crux of the challenge, all in all, is how to be respectful of the insights of race- and class-oriented theorists and, simultaneously, to avoid playing one against the other competitively. Little stands to be gained if, rather than bringing observations about race and class together to improve the lives of minorities and people of varied classes, the two perspectives are counterposed against one another, threatening to cancel out the gains of each. But where, now, does gender fit into the different ways of interpreting race this chapter has thus far suggested?

"Complexifying" Race through Gender

In discussing how the ideas about gender raised in chapter 1 fit into the ideas about race explored here, we proceed by taking up two respective queries. First, where does gender come in when trying to render the study of race more complex, and what is the risk of ignoring it? Second, has gender, historically, been ignored within some race-based perspectives? How can this be corrected? In exploring the first query – where does gender fit in? – we use two popular cultural representations, a contemporary film to which students in "Gender, Race, and Class" often responded both emotionally and intellectually, and a well-known literary example, namely, *The Autobiography of Malcolm X*.[51]

In 1991, the then 19-year-old filmmaker Matty Rich made a low budget film about life in the projects of Red Hook, Brooklyn. The film, entitled *Straight Out of Brooklyn*, opens with the main character, an African American man named Ray, breaking objects around his apartment and yelling loudly at his wife about the "white man" who has, through racial discrimination, prevented him from moving out of poverty.[52] The viewer quickly realizes that Ray's frustration has become redirected toward his spouse in the form of domestic violence. Their two children, Dennis and Caroline, cower in the back of the apartment, too afraid to intervene.

The movie shifts to Dennis' life as a teenager growing up in the projects. As he strolls along the Brooklyn Heights promenade on a date, he looks at the view of the Manhattan skyline – redolent of Wall Street and its riches – and tells his girlfriend Shirley about his determination to escape from Brooklyn's Red Hook projects across the river. He wants to realize the "American dream." Shirley is supportive but believes strongly that the traditional avenues of hard work and study will yield the desired result, yet Dennis is unconvinced. His father's experiences with racism in the

South, and his family's economic difficulties in making ends meet despite both parents working, belie the notion that through education he can overcome the disadvantages of being an African American youth from a poor family. This cynicism, combined with his desire to move Shirley and his family out of poverty, leads Dennis and two of his friends to become involved with a local drug dealer.

At the same time, *Straight Out of Brooklyn* continues to tell us more about Dennis's father and mother. His father Ray, who works in a gas station, is shown being demeaned by two white men, his boss and an impatient customer. The filmmaker explains the origin of Ray's indignation, showing how explicit racism undermined Ray's aspirations to become a doctor in his youth. Concomitantly, we see a gentler side of Ray: his efforts to share music with his son one afternoon, telling him how he used to dance; the happier side of his relationship with his wife as, one day too, we see them dancing together, before his frustration turns to anger. His wife's situation is also difficult in related but different ways. In addition to raising her two children, she has worked as a domestic for white women; in this respect, she fits within the framework provided by Judith Rollins in *Between Women* (see chapter 2). A white social worker who has previously placed her on domestic work assignments refuses to refer her for a job because she has a black eye (following a bout of domestic violence), even though she is in desperate need of money. Rather than understanding more sensitively (and multi-dimensionally) the complicated situation in which the mother finds herself, the boss at the employment agency sends her home without pay.

By the film's end, Dennis and his friends have tried to rob the drug dealer with whom they have become enmeshed. The drug dealers are out searching for Dennis just as, following a dreadful beating she sustains at her husband's hands, his mother has had to be hospitalized for her injuries. Simultaneously, the father is out looking for his son. In a denouement that brings Greek tragedy to mind in its utter poignancy, the drug dealer shoots Ray dead at the very moment that his mother's hospital monitor shows that she, too, has been fatally injured through the intricate nexus of race, class, and gender hardships her entire family has endured. This tragic chain of events reflects a hierarchy of discriminations that the family has unwittingly reproduced, in ways both of and not of their own choosing. In the final shot, a screen note bemoans how bad things pass from generation to generation: "We have to change."

What, then, does *Straight Out of Brooklyn* suggest about the relationship of gender-based observations to race- and class-based ones? Clearly, the film illustrates aspects of class, race, and gender discriminations. In terms of class, the Red Hook projects where Dennis, his friends, and family live contain an extreme concentration of poverty. Indeed, at the time the film was made, the majority of residents had incomes below the poverty line, and high unemployment rates vied with crime rates. The "American dream" also figures into the "hyper-ghettoized" inner city world of the film insofar as Dennis' hope is to escape, and to bring his family "straight out of Brooklyn" along with him. But class is about as obviously entwined with racism as more abstractly academic depictions can assert: were it not for racism, Ray might have been able to achieve a working- or middle-class lifestyle. In this social setting, race and class biases are so interconnected as to be, if not analytically indistinguishable, visibly co-present, each adding to the problems the other one bequeathed.

To understand where gender fits in, though, perhaps we have to return to the A/B/C diagram that was introduced in chapter 1. Based on Chancer's book *Sadomasochism in Everyday Life*, this diagram suggests that social stratifications in American society are often reproduced through the simultaneously powerful and powerless positions in which people find themselves.[53] Thus, in *Straight Out of Brooklyn*, Ray exists in a relatively powerless class and racial position relative to the (wealthier) white man exemplified by his boss and an arrogant customer at the garage where he works. Simultaneously, though, he is in a powerful position relative to his wife, against whom his anger at his powerlessness is expressed. Analogously, one can imagine that the same white man who is relatively powerful vis-à-vis Ray may be relatively powerless with a corporate manager (let's say, for argument's sake, another white man) who might own a larger franchise of gas stations to which Ray's workplace belongs. Or, say, a working-class white person who feels powerless against an upper-class white person may take out his anger at a relatively powerless third party. This might happen among men (for example, working-class white men may express racism even though they themselves are quite powerless in class terms). Or, as we saw in chapter 2's example taken from Rollins' *Between Women*, a white middle-class woman may express anger at a black working-class domestic over whom she feels relatively powerful; at the same time, she may be relatively powerless in relation to her husband.

Thus, one can argue that stratified relationships that are layered in combinations and permutations of gender, race, and class distinctions are maintained through the frequent ability of powerless persons to displace their resentment at parties structurally situated below them, toward whom they can transfer their anger. This is mapped in the case of *Straight Out of Brooklyn* and *Between Women* through the A/B/C diagram presented below:

Straight Out of Brooklyn	*Between Women*
A white upper-class man	white upper-class man
B black lower-class man	white upper-class woman
C black lower-class woman	black lower-class woman

Another way of explaining a similar concept is vis-à-vis ideas presented by Australian sociologist R. W. Connell in his well-known work *Masculinities*. According to Connell, most societies contain different forms of socially valued, and socially devalued, displays of masculinity. The most prestigious form of masculinity is the "hegemonic" variety defined, according to Connell, as "the configuration of gender practice which embodies the currently accepted answer to the problem of the legitimacy of patriarchy, which guarantees (or is taken to guarantee) the dominant position of men and the subordination of women."[54]

But Connell also describes the co-existence of other forms of masculinities that exist in relation to hegemonic masculinity. For example, subordinated masculinity is the kind experienced by men who challenge the dominant or hegemonic form either through their behaviors and/or their attitudes. Thus, an instance of subordinated masculinity would be a gay man who, by his "deviation" from the normative dictates of "straightness" (that is, heterosexuality) is demeaned by other men including those in the hegemonic, complicitous, or marginalized positions. One can concretize this through an example: the beating and subsequent death of a young gay man named Matthew Shepard in Laramie, Wyoming on October 7, 1998. Shepard, a working-class white man was attacked, beaten, and left for dead by two white working-class males who seemed to fit Connell's "complicitous" category of masculinity: these men are not well-to-do in class terms, but they may have racial advantages by being white and gender advantages through the "straightness" they shared with hegemonic men. Shepard's horrible murder, though, brings sadly to life the consequences some men endure when in a position of "subordinated" masculinity. Therefore, once again, this example of homophobic violence fits within the A/B/C diagram:

A hegemonic white upper-class man
B complicitous white working-class man
C subordinated gay white working-class man

Note that, in this particular example, the A/B/C diagram shows that powerlessness experienced in regard to parties situated "above" turned against parties situated "below" can and does sometimes take place among parties of the same race.

In Connell's third type of masculinity, though – the one most readily applicable to *Straight Out of Brooklyn* – such turnarounds can be spurred by race-based as well as class-based experiences of relative powerlessness. Connell deems "marginal masculinity" the kind that is felt when men who are alienated by a sense of class and racial disadvantages exert power over women; they may even do so to an extreme or exaggerated degree (possibly, sometimes, even including violence) as a way of compensating for feelings of resentment and disrespect they experience in other social arenas. Thus one way of understanding Ray's violence against his wife is not only vis-à-vis the A/B/C conception but also, in Connell's terms, as a manifestation of his feelings of marginalized masculinity.

These concepts can also be used to explore the relation of race and class to gender as manifested in our second popular cultural example, *The Autobiography of Malcolm X*. This is a text often used in undergraduate classes that focus on a wide range of sociocultural issues and which we use in "Gender, Race, and Class" to discuss relationships between these overlapping but not identical dimensions of the social world. In the first part of the *Autobiography*, we learn of Malcolm X's childhood and adolescence. Malcolm's father was a preacher in the South who was brutally murdered in 1931 by white racists because he was a vocal supporter of Marcus Garvey and the Universal Negro Improvement Association (UNIA). Following his father's death, Malcolm's mother was too poor to support him and his six siblings. Indeed, an insurance company refused to pay the claim on a policy her husband had purchased, insisting that the death was a suicide despite the fact that the father was severely beaten, his skull cracked, and his body almost severed after being laid across train tracks. But, in the 1930s, African Americans in East Lansing, Michigan were ill-equipped to challenge an insurance company. Malcolm's mother, forced to go on welfare to support their family, was eventually declared an unfit mother and the children made wards of the state.

Malcolm then grew up with his aunt and uncle in a middle-class black-dominated section of Boston, Roxbury, where he started to date a "nice" black woman, Laura, whom he initially intended to marry. However, around this time, he also became involved in petty robbery and eventually began to date a white woman, later ending his relationship with the faithful and adoring Laura in favor of the blonde-haired Sylvia. The *Autobiography* goes on to describe Malcolm's arrest for robbery and the years he spent imprisoned. It was during these years that he converted to the Nation of Islam and dedicated his life to helping blacks fight against the "white devil" through political action. Tragically, the "Malcolm X" renowned in American history of the 1960s, who is frequently associated with the philosophy of black power, was assassinated in 1967.[55]

In light of this short history, where do race, class, and gender discrimination fit into Malcolm's life, and do we get any sense of their interrelationship? The *Autobiography* makes entirely clear how racial and class-based forms of discrimination affected Malcolm X's early life. Not only his father's murder but life in segregated Roxbury reflected the pervasiveness of racism in its many forms. In terms of class, his father's death plunged the family into a state of poverty. In terms of the race/class debates discussed earlier in this chapter, Malcolm X's conversion to the Nation of Islam and his subsequently expressed views suggest that he would have agreed strongly with Massey and Denton and Steinberg – that is, he would have sided with the race side of the race/class debate. For while his own experiences document the extent to which both forms of discrimination are harmful, Malcolm came to believe that racial biases were the most pernicious force.

But what about gender – where does this dimension of the social world fit given the course of developments in Malcolm's life? Certainly the story about what happened to Laura and Sophia involved racism: Malcolm, as he realizes in retrospect, was attracted to Sophia largely because she was white and because he had internalized invidious and socially created feelings of racial inferiority. Yet the story also involves the distinctive character of gender since the separating of "good" women from "bad," madonnas from whores, is a hallmark of patriarchal societies wherein double standards of sexuality have been imagined and enforced. Applied to this case more specifically, Laura was not only African American and working-class but a "good girl"; she was the one Malcolm would have married and settled down with to live in a traditional family. On the other hand, Sylvia represented not only whiteness and wealth but promiscuity, which is often associated with the stereotypical "bad girl."

Although his experience with these women reflects both racialized and gendered prejudices, racial discrimination was the only factor that Malcolm recognized as having played a significant role. Years later, he learned that Laura was heart-broken when he abandoned her as a youth; after a series of hardships, she eventually turned to prostitution and was unable to realize her girlhood dreams. Malcolm describes the considerable guilt he felt about this, making him more determined than ever to fight racism; once again, the issue of sexism was absent from his reflections on his attitudes toward women.

After Malcolm's transformation in prison and conversion to Islam, he married Betty Shabazz. When he reflected on this relationship, again, awareness of gender-based discriminations did not figure. Their marital relationship was traditionally gendered for religious as well as social reasons; with Betty staying home to tend to their children single-handedly and Malcolm undertaking political work outside, their lives exemplified the traditionally gender-skewed spheres explained in chapter 2. Of course, one can object that the feminist movement was not sufficiently developed during Malcolm's lifetime to have exerted the influence it might have later on a progressive political figure concerned about injustice. Indeed, one year when teaching "Gender, Race, and Class" at Barnard/Columbia, Angela Davis gave a lecture that broached precisely this question: had he lived to see the blossoming and multi-faceted feminist movement, would Malcolm X have become a feminist? Certainly, his philosophy of black self-empowerment – his belief that black people needed to organize themselves because no one else was going to do it for them – anticipated other identity-based social movements, such as feminism and gay rights, that likewise were based on self-empowering principles.

Whether or not Malcolm X would have become a feminist had he lived longer, by the late 1970s and into the 1980s many African American feminist writers were assailing a kind of "macho" they felt was problematic for all women across, but also including, diverse racial and ethnic groups. Indeed, popular cultural sources like the ones just analyzed – *Straight Out of Brooklyn* and *The Autobiography of Malcolm X* – crystallize the importance of this development by illustrating how protests against racism can take place while other deeply embedded discriminations, like sexism, remain unscathed. Returning yet again to the conceptual vocabulary of chapter 1 – gender discrimination cannot be reduced to a function of racism any more than (as we saw, say, through Judith Rollins' *Between Women*) racism can be reduced to a function of gender. Several African American feminists have made this clear by arguing not only against racial and class subordination but by calling attention to the way gender-based discriminations have contributed to the many biases minority women regularly encounter.

Classic in this regard was Michelle Wallace's *Black Macho: The Myth of the Superwoman*.[56] Written in 1979 and reissued in 1990, Wallace argued that black power of precisely the kind exemplified by Malcolm X was deeply steeped in sexism, in "machismo." As she writes of Malcolm X in particular, "Malcolm was the supreme black patriarch. He would provide for his women and children and protect them."[57] In her introduction to the revised version of *Black Macho*, though, Wallace also notes that, in retrospect, she regrets anything about the original work that could be construed to imply that "black macho" was distinctive. More accurately,

Wallace later contended, men of varied races – not just men who are black – hold and act upon their sexist attitudes.

After registering this caveat, Wallace proceeded to make an interesting and important argument about the effect of male domination on African American women in particular. Black families were broken up by slavery, Wallace emphasizes; as a result, men's ability to be breadwinners for their family, a conventional marker of many masculinities, was correspondingly undermined. This often left black women in a position where they had to fend for their families themselves; moreover, since gender discrimination often leads to using women as a cheap and lower-paid labor force, black women sometimes found it easier than black men to obtain jobs. Adding insult to injury, black women have thereafter often been blamed for being "matriarchs" who did not care for their men – an attitude, as Wallace notes, which ignores the historical forces that led women to assume this role as head of the family. In this same vein, Wallace also notes that in Daniel Patrick Moynihan's 1965 report on the black family, Moynihan "righteously and indignantly related the professional and educational advancements of the black woman to high juvenile delinquency levels, high crime levels, poor educational levels for black males." But rather than generating sympathy, Wallace notes that "just as black men were busiest attacking Moynihan, they were equally busy attacking the black woman for being a matriarch."[58]

Moreover – and here is the heart of Wallace's argument – black women often felt guilty about their experiences of dual forms of subordination. Obviously, they were subject to racial biases but, just as clearly, they experienced sexism: the traditional dichotomies between socially constructed "masculinities" and "femininities" affected them too. Think, in the examples provided above, of Ray's wife in *Straight Out of Brooklyn*, of Laura or, in a different context, even Betty Shabazz. In each of these cases, one can point to ways that race and gender biases acting separately as well as together affected their lives. But then think, too, of what it would mean for Ray's wife to join a feminist group devoted to helping women overcome domestic violence victimization. Not only might doing so enrage Ray (and likely worsen the violence unless she removed herself from their home), but her own guilt would also affect her ability to escape. In the film she patiently explains to her daughter, who is concerned about the violence her mother is experiencing at her father's hands, that Ray's anger and rage are the result of the racist assaults (psychological as opposed to physical) he suffers on a daily basis. For the mother, the beatings are a burden she must shoulder as a wife, given racism in society; she considers any resistance on her part a betrayal of her husband and failure as a wife. But this leaves detached observers to wonder why the wife feels she should be subjected to violence because her husband feels powerless against his oppressors; so, obviously, did she. Her oppression, confounded by gender, race, and class, also matters.

Perhaps, then, the historical significance of Wallace's *Black Macho* is her insistence – even amidst later caveats – that black women's multiple experiences of distinctive but overlapping discriminations did indeed matter. By extension, this text provides a strong argument that black women need feminist support as much as – if not more than – women who have experienced less complex and multi-dimensional forms of oppression.

By now, we have come full circle. We have looked at several ways of defining race as Omi and Winant suggested (by way of ethnicity, class, nation, and non-reductionistically, that is, as an important way of understanding social relations in and of itself). We have also sought to make race more complex by examining its relationship to class. This examination suggested that race- and class-based discriminations are closely intertwined; at the same time each should not be reduced to a mere function of the other. Finally, this chapter argued for the need to consider, as a matter of course, how racially based discriminations and gender-based ones interrelate. Here, again, gender, race, and class turn out to be closely entwined; at the same time each cannot be reduced to an effect of the others. At this point, though, our magnifying glass of sociological investigation may not have given class its full due as an analytic term that needs "complexifying" in its own right. This is the next chapter's purpose: we will endeavor first to define class on its own and then to explore its relationship, as we have done in previous chapters, to other modes of discrimination such as race and gender.

CHAPTER FOUR

Class Matters

When teaching "Gender, Race, and Class" at Barnard/Columbia through the 1990s, we consistently had the following experience. In the initial part of the course students were quickly responsive to hearing about gender from different angles, and perhaps especially about the social movement history of diverse feminisms. The study of race and its complexities also regularly sparked interesting and often passionate discussions, and we were struck by the strong interest students exuded in debating issues that involved gender as well as race-based injustices. But, when the course turned to class, something in the air subtly changed. Many students did not seem as engaged or compelled; even students who were working-class, or who referred to themselves as lower middle class, apparently felt that the subject did not relate to them Why didn't class matter?

For one thing, the locale was Barnard/Columbia where, regardless of whether students were working class or well-to-do, they often expected to become (or to remain) highly successful in class-based terms. Simply attending an Ivy League school like Columbia was experienced by many students as an entrée to the much heralded American dream; to many it signified, and offered, an opportunity for upward mobility. Consequently when Stanley Aronowitz and William DiFazio guest-lectured one year in "Gender, Race, and Class" about their book *The Jobless Future*, arguing that capitalism was not replacing the jobs it was destroying through the work process, students argued with these sociology professors; some students even seemed angry. For to suggest that good jobs were disappearing may have struck some students as destroying the *raison d'être* behind the hard work they were putting into their education (as well as undermining a main reason for their parents working so hard to pay their tuitions).

Other reasons for a relative lack of interest can be deduced that take us outside the hierarchical distinctions of academic institutions per se. Certainly, by the 1990s, social movements focused on gendered and racial discrimination had affected – if not directly, then indirectly – many students' lives. Affirmative action had taken hold in admissions and financial aid policies at colleges and universities around the country. Moreover, in virtually all genres and media, concerns about men and women's equality (or lack thereof) and about ongoing racism in American society were being aired in popular cultural venues. Students knew from their own experiences, and often from that of their parents, that gender and race discrimination were significant social problems: more than this, discussing these biases had become relatively legitimized.

But class? In the US context, to say that one was a socialist was comparatively less familiar; it sounded a little weird. For those who did not agree with Marx's ideas anyway, to call for radical transformation in class-based inequities was vaguely threatening; for students who sympathized with Marxist perspectives, it rang as utopian. On the other hand, changes in gender and in race could be made, and some degree of upward mobility actually achieved, without fundamentally transforming the three-dimensional classification system of economic differentiation – lower class/middle class/upper class – with which most students, and Americans, are familiar.

To be sure, returning to concepts introduced in chapter 1, the above paragraphs should not be taken as universal but, rather, as historically specific observations themselves. In the UK and in Europe, for example, for students and professors (or, for that matter, the general public) to be left-leaning socialists, or communists for that matter, seems comparatively "normal" given the more wide-ranging political parties and political perspectives they grew up encountering. Academics with such views would be in sync, not out of sync, with those people in many advanced industrial societies who regularly vote for labor, socialist, or communist candidates and parties. In the US context, on the other hand, efforts to stress class-based inequities between the "rich" and the "poor" have not necessarily aided political candidates' prospects. For instance, in the 2004 US presidential election, attempts by Democratic presidential nominee John Kerry and his running mate John Edwards to depict Republicans as the party of corporate privilege and power were not sufficiently resonant to win them the election. This may be, as Stanley Aronowitz suggests in his provocative book *How Class Works*, because Americans are often in a state of denial about the extent to which class affects them. According to Aronowitz, class may be rendered "unconscious" in the American social psyche even though "in every crevice of everyday life, we find signs of class difference; we are acutely aware that class plays a decisive role in social relations."[1]

Nonetheless, it is striking that on May 15, 2005, the *New York Times* entitled a series of articles that the paper prominently displayed on its front page "Class Matters." The authors of the first article in the series found that "Over the last three decades, it [class] has come to play a greater, not lesser, role in important ways."[2] On closer examination, systemic manifestations of class like wealth, quality education, and well-connected social networks seem to transcend merit and place those who are of lower socioeconomic class at a distinct disadvantage. This is supported by the finding that "Americans are arguably more likely than they were 30 years ago to end up in the class into which they were born."[3] In the 1970s 36 percent of families stayed in the same income quintile, whereas in the 1980s 37 percent, and in the 1990s, 40 percent did so.

Yet the vast majority of Americans appear unwilling to accept the idea that there are disadvantages to being born poor and advantages to being born rich that function independent of individual effort. In a nationwide survey conducted by the *New York Times* in March 2005, 80 percent of Americans surveyed answered yes to the question "Is it possible to start out poor, work hard and become rich?" Forty percent stated that over the past thirty years rates of upward mobility have increased; 35 percent stated that they have remained the same; 23 percent stated that they have decreased.[4] Whether or not we acknowledge it, then, class does matter in the American context. Moreover, the existence of a synergistic relationship between educational and occupational opportunities is hard to deny. For example, the authors found a decrease in the proportion of lower-income students at the "most selective" colleges.[5] Given that income and education level are highly correlated with each other, as well as health status and life expectancy, the potential effects of class may be significant.[6]

Moreover, even within the United States, one has to be careful to make culturally specific rather than across-the-board (and more universalistic) generalizations. For instance, while Kerry and Edwards lost their bid for power, it is crucial to recall that 48.27 percent of voters (to be precise: 59,028,548 Americans) voted for them. Then too, returning to examples that are based on academic teaching experiences, students at Fordham have responded to topics in "Gender, Race, and Class" differently than students at Barnard/Columbia. Since students at Fordham often came from working-class or lower middle-class backgrounds, they more readily responded to theory about, and studies that documented, economic inequalities in America. On the other hand, some Fordham students have expressed relatively more traditional attitudes about gender.

While these variations in attitudes and background among students are important to note, overall, we wish to concur with the title of the series of articles in the *New York Times*. Adapting the title of Cornel West's bestselling book, indeed, class matters;[7] it remains an inordinately crucial, if not *the* most crucial social divider both in the United States and around the world. Without serious attention to class and the hierarchical differences it produces and reproduces, the complexities of gender and racial divisions are difficult if not impossible to understand. On the other hand, to make reductionistic arguments about class – as though this were the only dimension that counts – is just as simplistic as to advocate the primacy of gender or race. This chapter will also seek to show how class is just as complicated as the other two social dimensions this volume explores, gender and race. Once again, the question of what we mean by class begs investigation since several paradigms provide different interpretations.

Following the same format as in chapters 2 and 3, this chapter is analogously organized around, first, defining class through three possible paradigms with which students may be more or less familiar: the Marxist paradigm; the Weberian paradigm; and, combining ideas originally promulgated by both theorists, ideas about class that have most recently been developed by French sociologist Pierre Bourdieu. After providing this overview of three different but related ways of looking at class, the chapter's second part turns to complications, to "complexifying," this material. Why and how are problems likely to arise in studies of class unless considerations of race are habitually figured in? Last but not least, what are the ramifications of omitting attention to gender from academic and political perspectives that accord primacy mostly, or only, to class?

Reflecting on Class through Three Paradigms

I   Starting with Marx

Whatever one's perspective, it is hard to disagree that the work of Karl Marx played a seminal role in giving birth to contemporary ideas about class. Moreover, starting here allows us to trace the outpouring of variations-upon-themes that have developed in and around the work Marx (and his chief collaborator Friedrich Engels) left behind. We begin, therefore, by reviewing four basic ideas about class taken from Marx's thought: (a) the fundamental notion of wage work that defines workers' position, along with Marx's definition of profit, exchange value, and the commodity form; (b) the concept of "ideology" as found in Marx's writings; (c) the concept of "base/superstructure" relations in Marx's work; and (d) the theory of the tendency of the rate of profit to fall under capitalism, which led Marx to predict that the capitalist system would suffer periodic crises and a tendency toward demise. For each of these four ideas, examples aimed at bringing these notions to life by showing their ongoing relevance in the US and internationally are provided.

By way of commencing this introductory overview of Marx's thought, it should be noted that distinctions are sometimes made between the "early" writings of Marx and the "later." In the former category are usually placed writings dubbed "humanistic" insofar as they discuss "species"-related needs and have a philosophical bent. Here, notably, would fall *The German Ideology* and the *The Economic and Philosophic Manuscripts of 1844*.[8] In the category of Marx's "later" writings are usually classified works that looked at the "economic" workings of capitalism: this is where the three-volume opus *Capital*[9] is often located in discussions of Marx's work. While this distinction has some merit, Marx's work is nevertheless treated as a whole in the pages that follow. For an argument can be made that the usual distinction between "early" and "late" Marx is theoretically unnecessary since Marx's "economic" writings are also informed by the philosophical and humanistic ideas he developed early on in his writing. Similarly, it can also be argued that Marx's early writings suggest critical analyses of capitalism to come later.

(a) Wage labor and profit under capitalism

From reading *The Communist Manifesto* in high school, students often recall Marx's famed assertion that all societies have been class societies. By this usage of "class," Marx referred to a key distinction that can be made between parties who possess the means of production that bring them wealth in a given society, and those who possess little or nothing. Put very simply, this distinction is one between the "haves" and "have nots" of any society. However, while this "have" and "have not" distinction has been a prominent one in virtually all prior societies, Marx traced the way class divisions have manifested themselves in various incarnations from one historical period to another. Thus, as Marx detailed, class divisions in Ancient Rome differentiated between patricians and slaves; in the Middle Ages and feudal society, the main division was between landowners (who were often aristocrats) and serfs; in modern capitalism, the major division became that between the bourgeoisie (or capitalist class) and the proletariat (or working class).[10]

Evidently then, returning to the core concepts promulgated in chapter
1, Marx was firmly opposed to universalistic notions; apparent throughout his writings is an insistence on historical specificity. Then too,
for Marx, class was more than just an idea; it referred to "material" and
"real" divisions of society that are apparent in the patterned ways wealth
becomes distributed and is maintained over time. On the other hand, Marx
did not believe class divisions had to exist forever. Indeed, his analyses of
capitalism pointed to the possibility that, for the first time in human
history, this system's dynamic capacity for technological innovation
might create the "material" conditions to do away with scarcity: in
theory, it was possible to feed, shelter, and clothe everyone. This potential
meant that at least the material basis for class divisions themselves could
be overcome; class could "wither away." Yet, whether revolts against
capitalism succeed so that a more egalitarian communist or socialist
system comes to take its place, is not "determined" by nature but by
people's own activities and practical agency. As we will see below, this
broaches complicated questions of ideology that can diminish or increase
the chances of post-capitalist revolutions ever occurring.

But let us go back: if the character of class changed from Greek and
Roman societies through feudalism and capitalism, what is distinctive
about the latter? In other words, where we are now? According to Marx,
one way to define class relationships under capitalism was by asking
whether people live on wages or on profits; indeed, the very existence of
wages and profit, for Marx, is distinctive to and about capitalism. Prior to
the Industrial Revolution, barter relationships predominated: people
would simply exchange one desired item for another, for example, a goat
for a large quantity of vegetables and feed. With the rise of capitalism,
though, common currency – money – was also born: thereafter, everything could be exchanged in terms of quantifiably equal, and universally
recognized, coins or notes. This also meant that for the first time in
history, capitalism also generated a distinction between *use values* and
exchange values.[11]

Use values are manifest in bartering relationships wherein items are
transferred between people on the basis of, quite literally, their utility
or functionality to two parties. In a bartering relationship, one might
exchange a much needed cow for a much needed horse; it was how one
employed these items that mattered. Use values predominated in pre-
capitalist eras, and referred to (say) the value of a tomato as a vegetable
that one ate. With the rise of currency and market relationships under
capitalism, though, a tomato was no longer thought of functionally but in
terms of the price this vegetable could fetch if exchanged on the market.

Analogously, a coat ceased to be thought of primarily as a useful item that kept one warm in the winter time (its use value) but also as something that had a monetary cost or price (its exchange value). Note that these concepts began to become of a piece, to interweave with one another, since capitalism uniquely produced a society based on the commodity form. A commodity is an item that can be exchanged in the marketplace for money. As political scientist Marshall Berman titled one explication, paraphrasing Marx, under capitalism "all that is solid melts into air" as everything becomes perceived and evaluated, objectively and subjectively, in terms of exchange relationships. Nothing seems to have value on its own any longer but only vis-à-vis its value in money, in the marketplace, and as a commodity.[12]

At this point, the historically specific meaning of wages can also be explained since under capitalism, for the first time, even one's labor becomes a commodity; workers sell their services in exchange for a particular sum of money paid, as has often been the case, by the hour. According to Marx, capitalists have historically paid only subsistence wages: this refers to the amount a worker needs to reproduce herself/himself and her/his family through the provision of food, shelter, clothing, medical care, and so on. In a contemporary sense, "minimum wages" are paid to workers that may or may not prove enough to live on. But even people who in the United States tend to be referred to as members of a broadly defined "middle class" could be viewed as workers (or as members of the proletariat) if we adopt from Marx a definition that equate this group with wage-earners.

But what, by contrast, is profit – this being another critically defining feature of capitalism as a historically specific system that organizes the distribution of social wealth and services? Whereas the landowning class lived off the land under feudalism, under capitalism, the bourgeoisie lives off "profit." As a merchant class (again, referred to by Marx as the "bourgeoisie") grew under capitalism, this class used or borrowed money to buy factories that slowly began to produce a wide range of commodities that would be sold in the newly developing capitalist marketplace. From monies earned through the sale of commodities produced in the factory, the capitalist would have to pay for the cost of the factory itself (or for rent), for raw materials, and, of course, for what labor cost him in wages. The monies left over after all these expenses had been paid – usually a sizable amount and certainly many more times the amount workers earned in wages – went to the capitalist as "profit."

Marx also subscribed to the labor theory of value. According to this theory, it is the workers – not the capitalist – who have actually produced the value of goods later sold on the marketplace. Their collective effort has culminated in the commodities that factories and other capitalist work-places sell; yet it is only the capitalist, often altogether absent from the work process, who substantially profits. For Marx, then, capitalism involves the "appropriation" of value from workers who are paid only wages (and often paltry wages at that). This places Marxist theory very much at odds with conventional economics as taught, say, in business schools. For, as a "mainstream" economist would likely argue, it is not true that the capitalist has done nothing. Rather, such an economist might argue, substantial risks were entailed in investing and running a business; profits, by this logic, are not by-products of exploitation but deserved paybacks to people who have taken risks.

But whether one agrees with the Marxist or the conventional interpretation, suffice it for now to say that Marx himself was obviously depicting the workings of a particular economic system. For Marx, to the extent that capitalism was a system in which commodification and exchange relationships pervaded everything (including both the objective world and workers' inner subjective feelings), it was likely to become increasingly exploitative. Here, the continuity referred to earlier between the thinking of the "late" and the "early" Marx can be demonstrated: whether people feel alienated from within (as Marx described in his youthful "humanistic" writings), or partake of economic processes that led to their own products being appropriated from without (as Marx described in the "economic" volumes of *Capital*), the system which bred both struck Marx as contaminated at its core. For under capitalism, as Marx argued in both *Capital* and (say) *The Economic and Philosophic Manuscripts of 1844*, people begin to think not only of objects but of themselves and each other as commodities.[13] Everyday language came to contain phrases like "How can I best sell myself?" which can refer to interpersonal relations in a singles bar or how one writes a résumé. For Marx, such a system was highly problematic insofar as, within it, the use value dimension of human relationships – the values of love, of friendship, of work, of spirituality, none of which can be translated into economic exchange values – started to be replaced by more exclusively instrumental relationships. Yet, it is basic non-instrumental values that are at the heart of our "species being," potentially allowing us to live in harmony with each other and the world.

(b) Ideology

Once a world of wage labor and profit, and of commodification, has been established under the structural aegis of capitalism, other experiences at once "subjective" and "objective" follow suit. Key to Marx's theoretical system was a particular usage of the term "ideology": this can be defined as a set of beliefs or values that serve, in effect, to maintain and reproduce a given set of social relations. By our adaptation, ideology can be used to perpetuate a racial system (take, for example, the apartheid system as it used to exist in South Africa) or a gender system (take, for example, the relationship between a hypothetical batterer and a person who is battered). In the first example, it would be ideological for whites to say that blacks were inferior in intelligence to Caucasians. This promulgates beliefs aimed at justifying the maintenance of a situation based on racial dominance and subordination; as a result of these beliefs, the dominant position of people who happen to be white is more likely to be maintained. In the second example, it would be ideological for a husband who was battering his wife to proclaim loudly that she could not take care of herself. This belief would make his partner more likely to stay in their relationship, thereby rationalizing and perpetuating a small-scale system that accords him greater power in contrast with her relative powerlessness.

How does ideology operate, though, when it comes to class? Here, one can provide a variety of possible examples in a specifically American cultural context. Starting with observations about the United States made by Alexis de Tocqueville, a deeply embedded cultural ethos in the United States has been individualism. This is the notion that, in America, one can and should rely on oneself rather than the larger social community for survival and enrichment.[14] This explains longstanding cultural differences between the United States and Europe in terms of willingness to provide welfare supports from the state. What this means is that should an individual fail to procure a job – even in situations where, logically, more applicants exist than employment opportunities – he or she may internalize that difficulty, blaming themselves rather than the structural social and economic conditions that actually created this situation. This can be seen as ideological in the Marxist sense insofar as the cultural notion of individualism, in effect, contributes to the maintenance of a capitalist system. Insofar as people blame themselves rather than the "system," they are less likely to protest or to seek out organized ways of altering the situation; they may become more inclined to view their predicaments in psychological terms.

Relatedly, in his famous essay "Social Structure and Anomie," sociologist Robert Merton contended that the "myth of Horatio Alger" has been highly influential in American culture.[15] While Merton does not use Marxist concepts explicitly, his essay can be used to exemplify the notion of ideology associated with this tradition of class theorizing. According to Merton, the rags-to-riches notion that anyone can "make it" in America, no matter how poor one is on arriving from foreign lands, is a deeply embedded ethos; in a Marxist sense, this ethos works ideologically, and quite brilliantly, to keep American capitalism in place.

More precisely, Merton wrote that every society has legitimized means and legitimized goals; these must exist in a reasonable relationship with one another if people are to be adequately satisfied within, and not revolt against, a given society. In the United States, the legitimized goal to which most people aspire has been power as measured through money and wealth; concomitantly, the legitimated means of obtaining money has been hard work and education. Again, as the myth of Horatio Alger states, everyone who comes to America – no matter where they immigrated from, and no matter how poor they are when first arriving – has the possibility of realizing the "American dream" of wealth and prosperity.

But central to Merton's argument is that most people do not actually realize the American dream of wealth no matter how hard they try. In 1999 the top 1 percent of US households possessed 39 percent of the country's total wealth, whereas the bottom 80 percent of households possessed 15 percent of total wealth.[16] Thus, believing that anyone can make it in America may serve to keep people from becoming angered at actual disparities between the means they follow and their frequently unrealized dreams. Ideologically speaking, if someone doesn't become rich, it is because they didn't work hard enough or were not good enough. Note that this ideology is simultaneously individualistic and political in its implications; it turns perceived discrepancies between myth and actuality against the self rather than against the society.

Consequently, as Merton suggested, many people use various cultural adaptations which operate like defense mechanisms with a sociological twist. One such adaptation is that of the "ritualist": this is someone who adheres to the legitimized American means (accepting low-paying and often low-status jobs) even if they do not attain the legitimized American goal (wealth). According to Merton, the ritualist may compensate for the indignity of not realizing the desired goal through mechanically (or ritualistically) taking pleasure in the bureaucratic tasks he or she performs.

Virtually the opposite cultural adaptation is played out by someone who fits within Merton's "innovator" category. This category refers to someone who tries to achieve the socially legitimized goal of wealth through illegitimate, i.e. illegal, means. Merton came to the conclusion that high rates of "innovating" were likely to occur in the United States precisely because the same goal (wealth) is held out to everyone regardless of race, class, or, for that matter, gender. At the same time, as indicated by the statistics on the distribution of wealth cited earlier, not everyone is likely to realize this goal. Because of this contradictory situation, Merton argued, one can explain high rates of criminal and deviant activity in the specifically American context. Indeed, American history is rife with examples of ethnic groups who have turned to organized crime and gang activities precisely because they perceive a basic unfairness. On the one hand, they had been told they could "make it" in the US; on the other, their experience of myriad discriminatory obstacles had come to belie their expectations. Indeed, one after another ethnography of American gangs – from Terry Williams' *The Cocaine Kids* to Martin Sanchez Jankowski's *Islands in the Street* – has borne out Merton's thesis. Overall, then, American cultural ideology results in many people's willingness to accept – and to internalize (blaming themselves rather than the social system) – the means/goals disparities they experience. Moreover, from a distinctively Marxist perspective, their doing so helps to keep the capitalist system in place by defusing challenges that might otherwise be threatening.

(c) Marx's notion of base and superstructure

But how do ideologies under capitalism come to be powerful and to exert so much influence? One way of responding is by way of illustration, drawing on a base/superstructure model that grows out of Marx's ideas. Let us imagine mapping Marx's notions in visual form as follows. In the "base" of this drawing – which can be taken as at the root of the capitalist system – is the fundamental class distinction that persists between capitalists/bourgeoisie (who, as explained above, live off profits) and workers/proletariat (who live off wages; note that this obviously includes the vast majority of Americans, including many members of the middle class). Marx would argue that this fundamental, indeed basic, class division influences a whole world of other institutions that develop in the superstructure (literally, above the structure) of a capitalist society. In this respect, Marx's theory was totalistic, endowed with the capacity to explain a host of social situations that go beyond "economic" relations narrowly defined. Thus relations in the family, in the media, in politics – indeed, virtually all social relations – can be traced back to class relations at the base as suggested below.

Base/Superstructure Analysis

Media Politics Education Technology State/Police Family Religion

Capitalist/Bourgeoisie   Worker/Proletariat

The significance of this schema derives from its ability to explain, in a way that is vivid and anything but abstract, a host of everyday experiences that have been greatly influenced by class. Take the media as a starting point for exemplifying the influence of the base on the superstructure in capitalist societies. Edward Herman and Noam Chomsky have long noted a close relationship between the growth of multinational corporations and the subsumption of a vast variety of media.[17] Newspapers and magazines are quite likely to be owned by corporations, and to be run by billionaires like Rupert Murdoch. In the realm of television media, one does not have to think long or hard to realize that programming decisions are made by corporate sponsors who are likely to favor programs that seem compatible with capitalist interests. Thus, it is not likely that there would be a television show on a major channel that features a happy family living and talking about the virtues of a socialist society: this is almost comical to imagine. On the other hand, it would be much too simplistic to say that contemporary capitalist popular culture simply reflects in the superstructure class divisions that are extant at the base. For example, movies that are critical of some aspect of capitalism may be well funded if they promise to be profitable. How, otherwise, would Michael Moore have been able to produce films that have been consistently critical of advanced American capitalism from *Roger and Me* to *Bowling for Columbine* and, most recently, *Fahrenheit 9/11?* At least to some extent, as argued in more detail below, workers can influence the character of representations they are interested in seeing – an effect that may take popular culture in interesting, and not always predictable, directions.

Obviously, this base/superstructure relationship of influence rather than "determination" can be extended to understand the sway of class on other social institutions besides the media. Take American politics. We have often asked students, rhetorically, how they would characterize the class background of members of the US Senate and House of Representatives: do they think politicians' class backgrounds are one-third lower-class, one-third middle class, and one-third upper-class elected officials? Clearly, the distribution is not even to this degree. Students immediately recognize, as would most Americans, that members of the upper class are very disproportionately represented in politics. Running for office in the United States is presently an inordinately expensive proposition, requiring large numbers of well-to-do corporate supporters who are not likely to fund oppositional – say, openly socialist – candidates.

Moreover, once politics comes to be disproportionately dominated by members of the upper class, the very content of law is likely to be class-influenced in turn. Take, as an example, criminal penalties for various categories of crime in the United States. Criminal laws like New York's draconian Rockefeller drug laws have had a decidedly skewed effect, leading to a very disproportionate imprisoning of people who are poor and/or working class; on the other hand, corporate crimes often become matters of civil law and have tended to be prosecuted much more leniently.[18] This is not surprising insofar as the upper class obviously has more input into the contents and forms of law and, according to Marxist theory, are unlikely to make laws that run counter to their own interest. On the other hand, again, this should not be interpreted over-simplistically. In the US between 2002 and 2005, high-profile crime cases included ones against corporations: the case of Enron, and the issues of corporate corruption, became virtually a household reference. Similarly, the case of celebrity household designer Martha Stewart captured immense media attention when she was tried over a seemingly minor corporate-related infraction and sent to jail. Once more, the relationship between the base and superstructure should be theorized as a tendency rather than a determinative rule.

In the field of education, a relationship between base and superstructure is also easily exemplified. As most educators in the US and other Western European contexts are aware, students of upper- and upper middle-class backgrounds are disproportionately admitted to the very best colleges and universities on both sides of the Atlantic. In the United States, such advantages may stem from preferential treatment given at Ivy League schools like Harvard, Princeton, and Yale to children of prior graduates. But the reproducing of such advantages also stems from prior advantages in the educational system: children of the well-to-do are more likely to be sent to preparatory schools that train them in the skills, like taking SAT tests, which elite universities require. Indeed, one can argue that Scholastic Aptitude Tests (SATS) are class-biased insofar as children who attend poorly funded schools in poor neighborhoods are less likely to learn how to succeed at such tests. Analogously, their parents are less likely to be able to afford, or even to know about, companies like Stanley Kaplan and Princeton Review that exist to bolster students' scores on standardized tests. In other national contexts – take now, as another example, Britain – schooling is known to be notoriously class-stratified. A young person's chances of attending a prestigious university like Cambridge or Oxford are either helped, or impeded, by their class position at birth.

Nor is it difficult to exemplify the base/superstructure relationship of influence in other areas, for instance, in science and technology. People in powerful class positions have disproportionate ability to influence funding and, by extension, the direction and scope of supposedly "objective" research. Then, too, "subjective" or "private" everyday life experiences are also affected by Marx's theorized base/superstructure relationship.

Within the social institution of the family, it is easy to glimpse what sociologists Richard Sennett and Jonathan Cobb have termed "the hidden injuries of class."[19] Clearly financial problems within families are greatly affected by their resources: this includes whether or not housing can be easily provided, toys purchased, or vacations taken, and whether basic needs like medical care can or cannot be met.

In the realm of religion, at once public and extraordinarily intimate and individual, Marx also envisioned a relationship to underlying economic inequalities apropos the base/superstructure diagram. In much quoted passages of *The Communist Manifesto*, Marx famously argued that religion was quintessentially ideological: it was an "opiate of the masses," he complained, keeping people passively satisfied with conditions not of their own making.[20] Precisely because religious beliefs allow people to feel that after death they may go to heaven, and therefore to a salvation preferable to life, an "ideological" purpose is served: they turn their dissatisfactions inward rather than outward against intolerable life conditions. Thus, material class divisions at the base of society arguably affect the appeal of an array of religions that promise salvation, from Catholicism to Protestantism, Judaism and Islam – an appeal that, in contemporary societies, continues to be enormously relevant.

One point made above deserves reiteration: again, Marxist theory can be said to show a relationship of strong influence between the base and superstructural institutions, but an influence that is not necessarily determinative.[21] Thus it would be much too facile, and ignorant of a vast literature that has developed in literary criticism and cultural studies, to argue that representations simply reflect the interests of capitalists: culture and popular culture are far more complex. Not only Michael Moore's movies but many other American films from *Wall Street* to *Titanic* to *Silkwood* have bemoaned both corporate corruption and class-biased hierarchies. Similarly, while some television shows overtly hold out the hope that anyone can become a millionaire (included here would be the crassly titled *How to Marry a Millionaire* and reality shows like *Survivors*), others, from *NYPD Blue* to *Roseanne*, make working-class life much more their central focus, sometimes taking issue with the values (or lack of values) of upper-class existence.

Nor can or do base/superstructure relationships in capitalist society prevent large-scale protests against capitalism from occurring. Critiques and protests have often developed within educational institutions themselves (including, of course, at elite universities). As already noted, some films and books that critique capitalism or the hypocritical character of capitalist culture are economic "hits" for the companies who produce or publish them. The films directed by Michael Moore mentioned above are a case in point. Likewise Barbara Ehrenreich's book *Nickel and Dimed*, which bemoans the low pay and poor working conditions people experience under American capitalism, became influential, remaining on the *New York Times'* bestseller list for over a year and a half. In complicated fashion, then, these popular culture vehicles both undermine capitalism and comprise profit-earning ventures themselves. This raises the difficult but provocative question of which tendency is stronger, the self-preserving or self-destroying aspects of capitalism, and brings us to a fourth and final point in this overview: Marx's notions of crisis and the tendency of the rate of profit under capitalism to fall.

(d) Marx's theory of crisis

Once more, the so-called "early" and "late" Marx emerge as interrelated aspects of this theorist's work overall as we turn from capitalism's operations as a system based on wages and profits that affects most if not all superstructural social institutions (and relies greatly on ideological influences to reproduce itself), to tendencies and "contradictions" that pave the way for that system's possible destruction from within. The term "tendency" is important here: many students, when they first learn about Marxist theory, may not understand that Marx did not think socialism would *necessarily* arise out of capitalism. Rather, Marx wrote of propensities he observed that might, or might not, come to pass depending on a host of contingent historical factors and on the relatively independent perceptions and actions of individual and social agents.

Marx's theory, though, entails perceived structural problems that are likely to mark capitalism as a dynamic system in flux that goes through cyclical crises. One can understand Marx's theory of crisis as a step-by-step argument that starts with the social fact of a certain number of capitalists who are in competition with one another in a given industry. For Marx, this is a structural and definitional given: capitalists seek to maximize profit and, in so doing, will try to come up with new innovations and technologies that can outdo their competitors. Here, an important point should be emphasized: Marx viewed capitalism with disdain and admiration at the same time.

On the one hand, he anticipated that the innovative drive of capitalism would bring scientific and technological advances (that this prediction materialized can be exemplified, in contemporary contexts, by the development of computers and robotization). For the first time in human history, then, Marx thought it possible that human scarcity could be done away with. On the other hand, the tendency of capitalism was to become increasingly barbaric over time, its main motivation clearly profit rather than the meeting of human needs for survival and fulfillment. Consequently, people working in a capitalistic system are likely to become more and more financially insecure; larger and larger numbers are likely to become proletarianized wage workers, or anxious about their economic situations even as members of the so-called middle classes. But exactly why did Marx believe that capitalism – with its advantages and disadvantages – would be crisis-ridden in a way that pointed toward its own dissolution, that is, socialistic relations eventually coming to replace the older system with a more humane alternative?

Let us continue with Marx's step-by-step argument. Once capitalists are in a competitive relationship with one another, one entrepreneur is likely to invent something new. Thereafter, in order to survive, other capitalists have to follow suit; this is not a matter of individual choice but a structural imperative if Capitalist A (as we could call him or her) is to survive. Take, as a more specific example, the following easy-to-relate-to situation: in the computer industry, one company suddenly develops a new innovation, namely, a laptop computer. Other companies now feel forced to follow suit if they are to compete successfully with their competitors. But, to follow suit, they have to put more money into developing the new product and coming up with their own line of (say) laptop computers; they will have to invest in what corporations call their "research and development" (or R&D) departments. This means that a new cost has now been introduced into the production process. Consequently, the costs of a particular capitalist running his or her business – which regularly include rent, materials, depreciation of machinery, and, of course, wages – have a tendency to increase over time. Correspondingly, the profits of Capitalist A are likely to decrease. Recall from the earlier part of this overview of Marxist theory that profits are the left-over monies on which capitalists live once other expenses have been paid. Now, in the context of his theory of crisis, Marx suggested that this amount tends to decrease over time in the face of intra-capitalist competition.

But what happens once the rate of profit falls? According to Marx's analysis, capitalists are very likely to want to bring the rate back up again so that their profit levels remain high. How can they do this? Numerous options are available but not all are likely to accomplish the goal. One possibility is to increase the price of one's product: the obvious flaw in this strategy, though, is that profits might then still go down given that other capitalists' prices will thereby become relatively lower and more attractive as a result. Another possibility might be to cut costs by producing less but, again, fewer products sold would result in ongoing decreased revenue. Therefore the much more likely measures for a capitalist to take, Marx observed, were steps that would have a strong effect on workers:

(a) a given capitalist might engage in "speed up," that is, demanding that workers produce more in a given period of time so that labor costs remain the same and output increases;

(b) a given capitalist might decide to cut wages, an action that might or might not be possible if taken against a workforce that was organized into unions, and who could strike in protest;

(c) a given capitalist (perhaps facing organized workers, or even if not) might move his/her workplace to a different part of the country or overseas in search of cheaper labor and materials; and/or

(d) a given capitalist might close down one or two factories, plants, or offices altogether.

Note, though, that the cumulative effect of these actions – cutting wages, closing workplaces, and/or moving out of the country to a region where workers have little option but to work for less – is to leave workers in a position of constrained financial resources themselves. This is because the steps that capitalists are likely to take to raise profits ignore workers' dual role as producers and consumers: paradoxically, with workers unable to buy goods because less money exists in their pockets, the rate of profit may fall again. In turn, capitalists alarmed at falling profits may repeat their actions, making the situation worse again – and so on. This downward cycle can result in a crisis in the capitalist system as a whole. Indeed, historical examples of the occurrence of such crises can be cited: an obvious instance is the often cited US Great Depression of 1929; other cycles of so-called "recession" if not depression have also been diagnosed through the 1980s and 1990s.

Nor does it take much sociological imagination to realize that some of Marx's predictions about capitalists' actions have come to pass. Michael Moore's film *Roger and Me* traced the effects on Flint, Michigan when one General Motors plant was closed. US manufacturers have also been leaving the Northeast for decades to find cheaper sources of labor and materials both in other parts of the country (in particular, the South and Southwest) and in other parts of the globe (from Mexico to Southeast Asia).

Once a downward cycle has been set into motion, Marx also theorized several possible outcomes. One possibility is that a socialist system might emerge out of crisis but if, and only if, workers are organized into unions which Marx believed could take on the running of society on principles that are much more democratic in economic terms. But Marx also emphasized that socialism was not a necessary and inevitable result: another possibility is that the capitalist system might correct itself. One way this could happen is if some capitalists in a given industry were to go bankrupt following a crisis; fewer capitalists would remain, with the result that these survivors could each grab a slightly greater piece of the total market (thereby increasing their profits) in a given industry. Once that happens and profits begin to increase even slightly, workers can be rehired and the economy will improve and start to come out of a slump.

However, assuming that capitalism is able to avert its own tendencies toward destruction in the way just described, an important consequence is that classes become, after each crisis, more and more unequal in terms of the numbers of people within them. For what happens to the former capitalist who went out of business? Perhaps he or she, no longer able to support himself or herself on entrepreneurial profits, will start to work for wages (albeit perhaps at higher than average wages as a middle or upper-level manager). Thus, at the end of each successive capitalist crisis, Marx concluded, more and more people are likely to have moved into the working class, and fewer and fewer remain capitalists: in sum, class disparities under capitalism become increasingly skewed. Those who labor as part of a broadly defined working class come closer toward comprising the entirety of a society, leading Marx to envision laborers as eventually a "universal" class.

Again, key to understanding Marx's ideas is the realization that, contrary to what has been called "vulgar Marxism," no mechanical or scientific law of history was being invoked as guaranteeing socialism's automatic transition into capitalism. Rather socialism's ability to replace capitalism as a new system that would be both economically and politically democratic depended on human will – that is, whether or not workers organized themselves into unions that could run society efficiently and fairly. In this sense, Marxist theory exemplifies what has been recently dubbed in social theory a "structure versus agency" debate. "Agency" refers to individual will and consciousness that is affected, but not rigidly determined, by social patterns of gender, race, and class. "Structures" involve institutionalized processes that are far more ossified and difficult to change. But, while a theory of individual agency is certainly suggested by Marx's ideas about class, the second and third theories of class to which we now turn elaborate far more on how, and why, problems arise unless both the dynamic possibilities of individual agency and the overbearing constraints of social structure are simultaneously given their due.

2   Continuing with Weber

Chapter 3 emphasized advantages incumbent on rendering theories of racial discrimination more complex by incorporating considerations of gender and class discrimination as well. In this vein, one can envision sociologist Max Weber – a figure in sociological theory whose influence is comparable to Marx's – as engaged in a process of "complexifying" ideas of class promulgated by the previously discussed classical thinker. We will focus on the ways that Weber modified two ideas of Marx's in particular, reflecting both Marx's influence and Weber's desire to differentiate his own ideas and body of work. One important distinction concerns how Weberian theory conceptualizes the base/superstructure scheme of class relations previously outlined. A second way of introducing Weber's thought, and showing its distinctiveness from Marx's, points us toward the former's theory of bureaucracy. Here, Weber's diagnosis of modern capitalism parts ways from Marx's, suggesting that bureaucratic structures would continue to pose an apparently insoluble problem even if capitalism was replaced by socialism. According to Weber, unless some solution to the problem of bureaucracy was found, even socialism might not bring greater human happiness for masses of people, as Marx had envisioned.

In *The Protestant Ethic and the Spirit of Capitalism*, Weber immediately acknowledged Marx's contributions to understanding the characteristic features and dynamic processes of contemporary capitalism. Yet Weber just as quickly took issue with Marx's notion of religion as an opiate of the masses. Rather than seeing religion as a social institution that simply supports and reproduces capitalism, Weber argued that capitalism emerged from a particular religion's response to its adherents' fears of death. In other words, if we cast his ideas in *The Protestant Ethic* in terms of the base/superstructure diagram when discussing Marx's theory of class, the result is to reverse the emphasis: rather than stressing how class relations at the base influence an institution of the superstructure (namely, religion), Weber's approach highlights how religion has historically affected the shape of economic relations at the base. Early on in *The Protestant Ethic*, Weber wonders why capitalism took root in the West but not in the East. What were the factors that led the Industrial Revolution to occur in Europe and the United States rather than in the Orient? On analyzing this question in close historical detail, Weber hypothesized that a critical distinction between these areas of the world was their different religious cultures.

Only in the West, Weber proceeded to argue, did a capitalistic ethos develop within Protestant religions that placed stress on hard work and industriousness. In China, and India, for example – that is, in the East – the dominance of Buddhist and Taoist religions encouraged leisure time and did not foster a fast-paced speed of development. By contrast, Protestant religions in the West developed cultural imperatives of the kind Weber quotes Ben Franklin as circulating, in the form of maxims, in the United States. These involved, for example, the belief that "time is money," "credit is money," and "money is of the prolific, generating nature."[22]

Even more specifically, Weber contended that not all Protestantism spurred on the growth of capitalism: it was Calvinism in particular to which many early capitalists in the West subscribed. Calvinism, like other Protestant religions, was based on a covenant of grace, not a covenant of works. A religion that is built around a covenant of works, like Judaism or Catholicism, allows people to ensure salvation by following particular codes of behavior (for instance, following the Ten Commandments or going to confession on a regular basis); as long as one adheres to such precepts, salvation in the after-life is ensured. On the other hand, a religion organized around a covenant of grace – for example, Calvinism – does not permit people to know whether or not they are saved. Some people are "predestined" for grace but, unfortunately, this cannot be known through a priest's intervention or assured simply by following prescribed norms of behavior. This left an individual Calvinist alone to ponder the question, "Am I one of the elect?"

Thus, Protestants in general and Calvinists in particular found themselves in a position of unrelenting anxiety and insecurity, not being sure who was saved and how to ensure one's own salvation. However, Calvinists also thought that building the world to ensure the glory of God was one way of making oneself, and others, believe in their own predetestined salvation. Consequently, Calvinists developed a religious ethos that was at once strongly work-oriented and ascetic in character. What is the relationship between this and capitalism? According to Weber, Calvinists concerned about their mortality would work incessantly on projects that would increase the value of the world; entrepreneurial activities like owning factories conformed perfectly to this specification.

Moreover, Protestant asceticism meant that once early capitalists made profits, these funds would not be put to sensual uses like taking vacations or buying commodities, from cars to fancy clothes, which were not strictly needed. Rather, Calvinist anxiety to ensure salvation meant that profits would not be spent but accumulated. Thus, the early Protestant who was Calvinistic in orientation would take profits and re-invest them in more factories and additional enterprises, thereby fulfilling one of the preconditions – that is, a tendency toward accumulation – that Marx himself observed to be a *sine qua non* of capitalistic development.

The significance of this approach to class is that, in the Weberian tradition, culture and religion are not simply separable from economics. Perhaps more than any other classical social theorist, Weber opened the door toward indeed "complexifying" class, and, as we will see later in this chapter, toward assessing its relationship with other sociological concerns. But there are other important respects, too, in which Weber's ideas about class diverged from Marx's and pointed toward further refinements in contemporary class theorizing.

In his three-volume work *Economy and Society*, Weber argued that not all class positions are valued equally by members of society: an important distinction needed to be made between class and status.[23] In contemporary societies, someone can have status without class and class without status. For example, in the former category would fit a professor whose income may not differ very much from the salary of a highly paid administrative assistant at a top-notch law firm. On the other hand, the professor's position may confer more status, in the sense of generally recognized social importance and the possession of relatively rare social knowledge, than the administrative assistant's. Another example might be an old well-established family (in European countries, perhaps one which had aristocratic ties) high in social standing and status but fallen on economically poor times (perhaps close to penury). Conversely, someone may have a great deal of money but not much status. Here, an example might be an organized crime figure or someone engaged in legal activities (perhaps a self-made, wealthy, but relatively uneducated man whose social standing may be viewed suspiciously in more genteel social circles). In these examples, wealth in class terms has not translated into, or ensured, that a party also possesses status.

Then too, theoretically, Weber called attention to the possibility that Marx's hopes for revolutionary transformation might be stymied by another observation that differentiates his ideas about class from those of Marx. In *Economy and Society*, Weber laid out his theory of bureaucracy. According to him, complex modern societies are unimaginable without the invention, and widespread use, of the bureaucratic form.[24] Bureaucracies are organized as pyramids, fanning out from fewer people in charge at the top of an organization to people performing ordinary and less responsible tasks at the bottom. But Weber's point was that, wherever one fits on the pyramid, bureaucracies are routined and rationalized to provide laid-out tasks, and to specify rules and regulations, in advance. By Weber's definition, they are organized by departments, involve specified tasks, use files for the first time in history, and are, above all, predictable. For Weber, these traits meant that bureaucracies offered an organizational form that was well suited to accomplishing complex tasks – namely, the distribution of goods, income, and services en masse – which are necessary if contemporary societies are to function efficiently. Indeed, according to Weber, chaos and uncertainty would abound in mass societies were it not for bureaucracy's distinctive advantages.[25]

Yet this very set of advantages was at the same time disadvantageous: Weber is known for his skepticism, and eventually his pessimism, toward the question of whether emerging capitalist societies could be transformed in a more humanistic direction. At the end of *The Protestant Ethic*, he referred to an "iron cage" in which human beings are likely to be entrapped once capitalism, founded on an ethic of unrelenting labor, was established. One reason the "iron cage" might be inescapable also relates to Weber's assessment of bureaucracy and its ramifications. In Weber's conception bureaucracies are, at one and the same time, the most efficient way modern societies meet their mass-based needs and a source of seemingly inescapable alienation. As Weber argued, the individual within a bureaucracy is like a cog in a wheel; he or she knows that, without this individual, the machine-like organizational structure will continue. Bureaucracy leaves little room for charismatic elements and spontaneity; in these respects, it tends to be inhumane.[26]

Yet Weber did not foresee any way in which the bureaucratic form, and the iron cage bequeathed by emerging capitalism, could be overcome: his theory does not contain any escape provision or mechanism. This obviously contrasts with Marx's theory about capitalism's tendency toward crisis, which creates revolutionary possibilities for an organized working class. Moreover in Marx's vision, following a socialist or communist revolution, the state – as a governmental entity necessary to bring about revolution, and to ensure its immediate success – would "wither away." But, Weber wished to counter-argue, why was this necessarily the case? All modern organizational entities, from corporations to governmental agencies through labor unions of workers that Marx believed could transform society, are structured bureaucratically. Once established, then, both states and labor unions become entrenched; they are hard to dislodge because invested in their own perpetuation *qua* bureaucracies. Again, for this dilemma, Weber had no solution. Still, the very logical and trenchant character of Weber's critiques gave an impetus to the development of other contemporary class theories that, while also influenced by Marx, marries aspects of both theorists to better understand the intricate operations of class in the late twentieth and early twenty-first centuries.

3 The Synthesizing Brilliance of Pierre Bourdieu

According to Loïc Wacquant, describing contemporary developments in class theory, a subtle change occurred from Marxist to Weberian theories of class.[27] For one thing, while the Marxist lexicon employs terms like appropriation and exploitation, writings on class in the Weberian tradition are more likely to use terms like inequality and stratification. Whereas the Marxist lexicon emphasizes the primacy of two classes (the capitalist and the working class), a Weberian approach focuses more on gradations between classes and can encompass what is presently an often three-tiered understanding of class (lower class, middle class, and upper class). Whereas Marx emphasizes objectivity and objective relations, Weberian theory shows greater interest in the subjective dimensions of individuals' experiences.[28] From all this, it can be concluded again that the role of culture in shaping people's perceptions of class – their willingness to accept, or to protest and try to change a given system of class relations – grew in theoretical importance from one thinker to the next.

But we turn now to a more contemporary approach: the work of Pierre Bourdieu, which draws on both the Marxist and Weberian legacies, focusing perhaps most explicitly on cultural factors that affect the production and reproduction of class inequalities. More than the Marxist tradition, and in this sense closer to the Weberian tradition, the ideas of Bourdieu leave theoretical room for taking gender and race into account as factors that interact with but cannot be reduced to a function of class. Probably Bourdieu's most well-known work on culture and class is *Distinction*. Here, Bourdieu described in rich social scientific detail how gradations of class position correlate with a wide array of cultural tastes such as music, clothing, eating habits, and the use of language and bodily gestures. To be born upper-class or lower-class was much more than an economic fact: it was a cultural fact as well. For example, as Bourdieu shows, a taste for classical music is not universally felt but socially acquired, usually in elite contexts. And, while people of lower-class or working-class origin develop different cultural tastes, the knowledge that upper-class tastes are dominant in society overall creates a desire for emulation that, at the "subjective" level here emphasized, has the effect of keeping "objective" class relations in place as well.

Bourdieu also believed that the enculturation of class takes place through the medium of what he called "habitus." This is defined in *Distinction* as "both the generative principal of objectively classifiable judgements and the system of classification (principium divisionis) of these practices."[29] Habitus can come to seem "natural" since it is so everyday, routine, and practical; however, it is as much part and parcel of class-stratified systems as more widely recognized manifestations of inequality. As Bourdieu writes, "inevitably inscribed within the dispositions of the habitus is the whole structure of the system of conditions."[30] This set of learned dispositions become, quite literally, part of ourselves; they are transportable from situation to situation and affect how we view, interpret, and negotiate the world. Moreover, "complexifying" Marx again, but in a different sense than Weber, Bourdieu suggests that habitus is negotiated in a range of social fields. Not only does stratification occur in the economy as conventionally defined but, as he argues, in social fields like the academy (see, for example, his study of this field, aptly titled *Homo Academicus*), the medical field, and the legal field. Each of these fields has its own principles of stratification that people learn to negotiate, making contemporary advanced industrial societies exceedingly complicated for the permutations of class and status possibilities they contain.

Famously, too, Bourdieu rendered Marx's notion of capital more complex. Bourdieu used the term "economic capital" to denote the direct forms of ownership of social wealth (through, say, stocks and bonds) that Marx meant by his use of the term "capital." Bourdieu also believed that social capital exists. This involves another form of wealth that individuals can accrue even if they are low in economic capital; social capital results from associations and connections built through "networking," a concept that has recently come to interest sociologists at Columbia University and elsewhere.[31] Nor is economic capital the same as the last most well-known form of capital introduced by Bourdieu, that is, cultural capital. Cultural capital itself can be of different kinds. One type is academic capital, which results from investing in the educational system. In other words, regardless of one's position in (economic) class terms, cultural capital of the academic kind can, through the building of credentials, affect future wealth and status.[32] Thus, as students quickly understand, getting college degrees and advanced graduate degrees have the effect of building cultural capital. At the same time, at each of these levels, stratified status hierarchies mean that (for example) bachelor's degrees from Harvard, Yale, and Princeton in the United States, or, in the United Kingdom, from Oxford and Cambridge, are likely to accrue more cultural capital for a particular social agent than those from local community colleges. At the PhD level, too, particular areas – from sociology to anthropology – will have "rankings," as will medical colleges, law schools, and business schools. Analogously, then, graduating from Harvard Law School or (in the area of business) from Wharton Business School is likely to bestow greater cultural capital than attending a medical or business school ranked lower on the status hierarchy of these respective fields.

Because Bourdieu's theoretical conceptualization of class represents an immense broadening beyond the nineteenth-century ideas of Marx, they allow us to see how habitus is affected not only by class position but by systems of racial classification and by gendered forms of acculturation as well. Indeed, as we will see in chapter 5, ethnographic studies such as those done by Philippe Bourgois – who was himself greatly influenced by the work of Bourdieu – attempt to incorporate gender, race, and class multi-dimensionally into the social worlds each writer portrays.[33]

But, before turning to these works in chapter 5, let us look at how both classic and contemporary understandings of class (the latter, again, already attempting to "complexify" the heritage of the former) are affected when we turn to the other social dimensions this book explores. We will look at two examples – racism in the labor movement and the relevance of gender bias to class experiences – that illustrate how class, too, cannot simply be reduced to a function of race or gender. Each of these dimensions is interrelated with, but yet to some extent separable from, the other insofar as it may have separable origins and sources. But is this thought, in theory, always taken into account in practice?

Complexifying Again: Avoiding the Reduction of Race to a Function of Class

Marxist theory calls for an organized union movement to fight and overcome the injustices of capitalism. Marx himself did not write much about racism, and how it might affect class-based organizing. Still, as Omi and Winant suggest, Marxist-influenced theories of class stratification tend to view racial prejudices in relation to their functional ramifications for capitalism.[34] Recall that racism was seen as useful insofar as it operates as a divide-and-conquer mechanism. Moreover, according to Omi and Winant, racial biases also serve to devalue some groups of workers over others, thereby creating a group of workers whom Marx called a reserve army of labor, people willing to labor at particularly low subsistence wages and sometimes to engage in strike-breaking. Yet the class tradition that Marx played a disproportionate role in promulgating devoted scant theoretical attention to Omi and Winant's definition of race as a "fundamental axis of social organization in the US," that is not reducible to any other social dimension like class or gender.[35] Hardly considered were examples where, precisely because it is relatively autonomous, racism persists even within a framework where class inequalities are already being questioned or have been lessened.

Several examples of this problem can be found in historical writings that have devoted attention to competitive feelings between workers. For example, historian David Roediger has written about hostilities among white workers toward black workers;[36] other historians have also developed critiques of racism among white workers in varied contexts.[37] Although these examples may seem to support Omi and Winant's interpretation by focusing on the beneficial effects for capitalism of inter-group hostilities, Hill has also written about racism among groups of workers who are not competing for jobs.[38] Racist sentiments may surface in situations where workers are in the same union, united by the same goals of better benefits and job security. Nevertheless, like many other members of dominant racial groups across class categories, white workers still express biases and prejudices that are hardly admirable. What this suggests is that underlying causes of biases need to be investigated multi-dimensionally, not only as such biases can emanate from economic hardships but as they can additionally express deeply felt antagonisms that might remain even if workers' economic conditions improved.

Other examples can be cited outside the US context. Ethnic and racial tensions obviously simmered beneath the surface of the former communist Yugoslavia, leading to bitter outbreaks of hostilities and violence between the Serbs and the Croats. It is hard to believe that these ethnic tensions surfaced only because capitalism was gone; much more persuasive is the argument that a long history of ethnic antagonisms preceded and post-dated communism in Eastern Europe, illustrating the importance of understanding race/ethnicity and class in their complex relationship with each other.

Unless we keep both class and race together in our minds, and conceive of them in a relationship of tension with one another, resulting perspectives on race and class become far too simplistic. But where does gender come into play in this analysis?

Yet Another Level of Complexity: Not Reducing Gender to a Function of Class

Since its publication, Barbara Ehrenreich's *Nickel and Dimed: On (Not) Getting By in America* has been required reading for sociology students in "Gender, Race, and Class" at Fordham University.[39] Students relate strongly to the book since, in order to get through college, most of them have engaged in exactly the kind of minimum-wage jobs that Ehrenreich details. A journalist rather than an academic sociologist, Ehrenreich details the social world with a richness and acuity that is reminiscent of a fine ethnographer's work. In her research for *Nickel and Dimed*, she left her middle-class lifestyle in Key West, Florida in order to investigate whether people can support themselves with minimum-wage work in the US. Not surprisingly, her major finding is that workers in America are grossly underpaid and can barely live on the salaries they earn. To get by, Ehrenreich herself was often forced to work two jobs, a task that frequently left her physically exhausted.

While *Nickel and Dimed* does not directly study the interaction of class and racism, Ehrenreich makes clear reference to this omission in a caveat in the book's introduction. She describes her decision to take minimum-wage work in three locales – Key West, Florida; Portland, Maine; and Minneapolis, Minnesota – that have overwhelmingly white populations. Her rationale was to avoid competing with minority workers to procure the jobs that are the subject of her investigation. Otherwise, as she argues, a combination of racial and class discriminations in many localities made it likely that a region's lowest paid positions would be disproportionately given to minority workers.

Thus, while not studying racism directly, *Nickel and Dimed* by its very design takes racism into account. Much less so, arguably, did Ehrenreich explicitly take gender into account. Gender can be added to her study but it is not, at first glance, interwoven with her primary stress on class. But how does gender apply? Obviously, Ehrenreich depicts a world of work wherein both men and women find themselves in dead-end, poorly paid jobs. Moreover, among the many jobs she took to get by in Florida, Minnesota, and Maine were several (for example, working as a waitress, a hotel maid, a house cleaner, and a nursing home aide) that are overwhelmingly occupied by women as a result of the traditionally gendered associations (between women and supposedly natural care-taking tasks) that are discussed in chapter 2. In other locations, jobs as maids have been disproportionately occupied by minority women due not only to traditionally gender-biased associations but also to the eagerness of middle- and upper-class (usually white) women to farm out such demeaned tasks associated with nature like housework and domestic chores (see, again, chapter 2).

Nonetheless, what Ehrenreich does not explicitly consider in this superb and clearly written indictment of class inequalities in America is just what it meant for her investigation that she was a woman. Even more to the point, what if she had had children? One quickly reaches the conclusion that, if she could not get by supporting just herself on minimum-wage pay, it would have been virtually impossible if she were a young woman – let's say, a single mother – with three children to feed, shelter, and clothe. What would she have done? According to Kathryn Edin and Laura Lein's study of women, *Making Ends Meet: How Single Mothers Survive Welfare and Low-Wage Work*, women in this position are left no choice but to supplement their incomes – if not by taking second jobs, sometimes by engaging in illegal activities such as selling sex, drugs, or stolen goods, obtaining additional money from family or friends, or getting assistance from churches or private charities.[40] For a mother of three, one route for survival taken by Ehrenreich – accepting a second minimum-wage job – might not be possible. In addition, she does not deal with related issues such as sexism among workers and varied kinds of sexualization that workers regularly experience. However, in *Genders in Production: Making Workers in Mexico's Global Factories*, sociologist Leslie Salzinger does a superb job of showing how work relations on the shop floors of Mexican transnational assembly plants – or "maquiladoras" – actually "produces" gendered workers because of assumptions about the character of masculinity and femininity that are brought from family contexts to workplace settings.[41]

While Ehrenreich's book succeeds remarkably well at bringing classical Marxist perspectives on class to contemporary life, it does not therefore give equal attention to all three perspectives on the social world with which this volume deals. This was not Ehrenreich's intention, nor do all studies by scholars, journalists, and activists need to take all three points into account. But, as the above examples of race and gender suggest, a certain degree of complexity in the social world may remain unaccounted for by virtue of not including multi-dimensionality. In the case of class-related writings that do not consider the significance of racism and gender, the omission may have the effect of making us ignore the extent to which fixing class inequalities – while crucially important – may not lead to the eradication of discrimination in general.

With this, we now turn to a concluding chapter aimed at coming full circle back to some of this book's opening questions. First, where and how can we understand complex biases differently as a result of looking at gender, race, and class both separately and in interaction with one another? Second, does it matter that we try to recognize that social biases have specific roots and motivations yet reflect common underlying prejudices? Last but not least, what analytic advantages ensue from taking all three dimensions into account? In response, chapter 5 investigates a variety of works that have attempted to synthesize gender, race, and class.

CHAPTER FIVE

Concluding Thoughts

In coming to the end of this volume, it seems appropriate both to summarize points covered theoretically in this volume and to assess, more practically, its implications for continuing to study these dimensions of the social world. Consequently, our concluding chapter proceeds in two parts: the first is devoted to providing an overview of the material already covered, and the second to considering this volume's pragmatic ramifications. Woven into both parts are references to, and examples of, the conceptual vocabulary introduced in chapter 1. These were the notions of social constructionism (as opposed to determinism), complexity (as opposed to reductionism), Chancer's A/B/C diagram of power and powerless relationships (which can be used to analyze how stratified relationships, including ones based on complex layers of gender, race, and class, are maintained and reproduced), and, as relates to social movement organizing, the concepts of coalition and identity-based politics.

By Way of Synopsis

By now the richness of each theoretical tradition already surveyed, in and of itself, should be apparent. Whole courses can and should be devoted to exploring the meaning of gender, race, and class, each in its own right; at the same time, looking at these dimensions together is analytically valuable for encouraging investigation into how each differs from, and yet relates to, the others. Returning to where we started, then, with gender: recall that we focused on three possible ways to define the term: sociologically, anthropologically, and through the history of feminisms as an unfolding and itself multi-faceted social movement.

1 Returning to Gender

A sociological approach has usually involved distinguishing gender from sex, with the former term referring to social and cultural constructions of the supposedly neutral, biological facts of the latter. However, an important contribution made by Judith Butler to the development of feminist theory has been her insistent questioning of whether this distinction is itself a sound one. For what are the biological "facts" of sex apart from our social and interpretive constructions? In *Gender Trouble* as well as in later texts, Butler inquired whether it is possible to find a beginning, or an end, to the sway of social constructions. Why is there necessarily something called sex that exists, as though untouched by our linguistic and conceptual efforts at describing it, "behind" gender?

Through her critique of this distinction, Butler at once contributed to and expanded sociological interest in the centrality of social constructionist perspectives for comprehending gender. At the same time, the world of gendered distinctions that Simone de Beauvoir and many others have described with a more or less explicitly sociological bent has everything to do with social constructionism of precisely the kind that interested Butler. Traditionally gendered distinctions between "masculinity" and "femininity" have tended to accord superiority to the former and inferiority, by contrast, to the latter. Indeed, as explained in chapter 2, caretaking jobs that continue to be dominated by women remain generally lower-paying than jobs (from police officers to surgeons to corporate heads) that have long been disproportionately occupied by men.

While this sociological approach to gender helped us to grasp *how* it has operated, a second and more anthropologically oriented approach to understanding gender concentrates on discovering *why* women came to be treated as "the second sex." One explanation for the demeaning of the tasks and occupations associated with women over history was provided by Sherri Ortner, who argued that a dichotomized association of femininity with "nature" and of masculinity with "culture" has characterized virtually all early societies. According to Ortner, most societies have looked to culture for projects that can overcome the uncertainties of nature and its concomitant associations with mortality; since women are associated with nature, largely due to their biological role in reproduction, they too were seen as objects to be controlled and dominated. For Friedrich Engels, drawing on the anthropological work of Morgan, the origin of women's treatment as secondary citizens developed simultaneously with the emergence of private property. Once surplus came into being and men sought to establish legitimate heirs, women were mandated to be monogamous so that paternity could be ascertained; from this, a double standard of sexuality developed, and women themselves became an extension of private property.

Third and last, though, we saw in chapter 2 that gender can be defined not only in terms of how it operates, or why traditionally gendered arrangements grew to treat women as secondary, but also through its relationship to the evolution of the now international feminist movement. Specifically, in the US context, liberal feminism initially devoted itself to establishing equality (drawing on the heritage of liberalism itself), whereas radical feminism spawned a rich theoretical literature that defined controls over women's bodies as central to the exercising of gender-based oppression. At this point, Shulamith Firestone's *The Dialectic of Sex* provided one example of reductionism, apropos the conceptual vocabulary proposed in chapter 1. According to Firestone, critiquing the theory of the origins of women's oppression as recalled above, Engels' approach was highly reductionistic. By positing that gender subordination arose only with the institution of private property, he overlooked the possibility – indeed, for Firestone, the probability – that sex class may have pre-existed economic class with the imposition of men's biologically based power over women.

With the development of Marxist and socialist feminisms, though, radical feminist approaches were themselves roundly criticized as having failed to give adequate attention to class-based as well as gender-based differences. Now it is the concept of universalism, as introduced in chapter 1, that can be illustrated vis-à-vis these feminists' dissatisfaction with the radical feminist concept of "patriarchy." How could patriarchy exist in the same way at all times, and in all places, these groups of feminists asked critically? Alternatively, Marxist feminists contended, it was crucial to examine exactly how class and gender intersected in historically relative and culturally specific situations. In this regard, socialist feminist Zillah Eisenstein coined the term "capitalist patriarchy" to denote the more complicated system she felt women and men live under at present.

Last but not at all least, black feminists including Bell Hooks, Michelle Wallace, and Patricia Hill Collins have called theoretical attention to the omission, even in class-oriented Marxist and socialist feminisms, of adequate considerations of racial discrimination that minority women also face. In other words, like Marxist and socialist feminists, black feminists also contributed to an ongoing process of rendering early feminist theories (as developed by liberal and radical feminists) increasingly more complex. Indeed, by now, a rich empirical literature has sprung into being that documents the complexity of gender, racial, and class-based discriminations that many women of color regularly encounter.

One powerful example is Judith Rollins' *Between Women: Domestics and Their Employers*, a work which showed that race cannot be reduced to a function of gender. To some extent, African American domestics and their Caucasian employers experienced commonalities *qua* women; on the other hand, the domestic/employer relationship showed the simultaneous persistence of distinctions "between women" on the also extremely relevant grounds of race and class differences. On the other hand, as Michelle Wallace's *Black Macho and the Myth of the Superwoman* shows (see chapter 3), gender cannot be reduced to a function of race either. Racial solidarity is vital to overcoming the ugliness of discriminations that are based on skin color; yet, by no means does it follow automatically that eliminating racism guarantees the evanescence of sexism within racial and ethnic categories. Rather, Wallace pointed out, "macho" attitudes have posed a problem for women within many racial and ethnic groups – including but not limited to African Americans – who have experienced, and fought back against, discrimination.

2   Returning to Race

Whereas we looked at three ways of defining gender in chapter 2, chapter 3 turned to four paradigms that are useful in thinking about race and racism: ethnicity-based theories; class-based theories; nation-based theories; and Omi and Winant's own concluding perspective, that is, that race is a "central axis" of social relations autonomously and in its own right. Drawing heavily on Omi and Winant's now classic *Racial Formation in the United States*, we elaborated on the history and content of each of these paradigms. For instance, as we discussed, the ethnicity paradigm is the oldest in the US context, conceptualizing race as one of many characteristics – culture, religion, language, territory, among others – that come to comprise a group's ethnic identity. But Omi and Winant are also critical of this perspective, providing the first of three examples of reductionism that one finds in this part of their work. For, if one thinks of race as simply one component of ethnicity, its historical influence may be seen as less determinative; one could end up arguing, as theorists actually did within this tradition, that racial minorities should just be able to "pull themselves up by their bootstraps" as have other white ethnic groups; they should be able to succeed if they only tried hard enough to do so. The problem with this formulation though, as Omi and Winant point out, is that the virulence of racism in US history has affected African Americans' lives – for instance, no other group experienced the institutionalized horrors of slavery – in ways that make comparisons with white ethnic groups' histories (who have not encountered that depth of discrimination) unfair and misleading. In other words, the ethnicity paradigm tends to reduce racism to a function of ethnicity.

Analogously, Omi and Winant contend that one of the other paradigms for defining race that they propose – that is, class-based perspectives – can also be criticized for its reductionism. Among several forms of class-based theorizing that have touched upon race, one of the most influential has been Marxist theories of class. According to Omi and Winant, Marxist theories have tended to perceive racial discrimination in terms of how it affects capitalism, and the possibilities of workers' organizing against it. For instance, if the white working class feels racial prejudice against blacks and Latinos, or if Latinos (say) should dislike people from China, this serves a "divide and conquer" function that is useful for capitalism's survival and reproduction. Precisely for this reason, though, this class-based approach can also be said to be reductionistic, reducing racism to a function of class: what is suggested here is that, if capitalism were done away with, racism would wither away in turn. Yet, as Herbert Hill and other labor historians have argued, the history of American labor shows examples of racist attitudes that may be more deeply embedded than is explicable solely in terms of people's working-class attitudes. By extension, it would seem that Omi and Winant's concern about establishing race as an autonomous social axis, deserving of consideration in its own right, is amply justified.

Another type of class-based theorizing about race is stratification theory as exemplified in the work of William Julius Wilson. According to Wilson's arguments in both *The Declining Significance of Race* and *The Truly Disadvantaged*, class-based inequities have displaced race in the post-civil rights era as the main determinant of African Americans' life chances in the US. Here, then, we find an interesting variant upon universalistic (as opposed to more specific) thinking insofar as a main policy implication of Wilson's research was his advocacy of "universal," class-based programs rather than more specific, racially targeted ones. "Universal" policies are those which, if enacted, would benefit all groups cross-racially; examples of such policies are universal health-care and child-care provisions, changes in macroeconomic policy (such as changes in rates of taxation), and job creation programs. Racially targeted programs include affirmative action, a policy Wilson did not so much oppose as question for its relative lack of efficacy in a country where a black "underclass" had come to live in strikingly impoverished conditions (or what Loïc Wacquant has called conditions of "hyper-ghettoization").

On one level, no doubt, Wilson's points remain extremely persuasive. On another, according to Omi and Winant, the problem with Wilson's perspective is that it underestimates the relatively independent strength of racism. In other words, providing another example of this concept, Wilson also tends to reduce race to a function of class. The counter-argument made by Omi and Winant, and which has also been developed at great length by sociologist Stephen Steinberg, is that universal policies might not, due to racism, be applied fairly across the board in practice. This led us in chapter 3 to review the so-called race/class debates that continue to place some social scientists on opposite sides of this issue. Turning again to empirical literature, we illustrated the race side of this debate vis-à-vis Massey and Denton's study of *American Apartheid*, itself a striking piece of research documenting that residential segregation, proceeding as it does on distinctly racialized grounds, is a major reason for ongoing poverty, disproportionately affecting minorities including African Americans in the US.

Drawing heavily on Omi and Winant's critiques of reductionism in these perspectives – in regard to both ethnicity and class-based theories, and also to nation-based theories that reduce racism to a function of space or territories within which racial subordination occurs – we also suggest, in chapter 3, that one need not choose either race or class as *the* major factor that has affected racial stratification in the US. Rather, as Loïc Wacquant has written (again, see chapter 3), both race and class are implicated at the roots of racism's stubborn perpetuation. Moreover, as that chapter concluded, perspectives that render the study of racial discrimination more complex by calling attention to the relatively independent role of gender (as does the perspective of Michelle Wallace in *Black Macho*, discussed above) are also extremely valuable: even if we could eliminate racism, sexism would not simply follow suit as though in a domino effect.

3   Returning to Class

Whereas chapter 2 looked at three ways of defining gender, and chapter 3 at four ways of defining race (and racism), chapter 4 returned to a trio of theoretical traditions within which class has been conceptualized: the Marxist tradition; the Weberian; and, most recently, the innovative ideas of Pierre Bourdieu (within this last category should also be addended the recent and also highly creative approach to class taken by Stanley Aronowitz in *How Class Works*).

Under the aegis of Marxist theory, we reviewed four fundamental ideas. One entailed, quite basically, how Marx defined capitalism as a system dominated by a profit-making class (obviously, the capitalist/bourgeois class) in which a wage-earning class (obviously, the working/proletariat class) experiences economically based domination. Here, too, we reviewed the distinction between use values and exchange values that led Marx to see the permeation of the latter as a hallmark of emerging capitalism. Secondly, we turned to defining ideology as a particular system of beliefs and values that serve, in effect, to perpetuate and reproduce extant power relations under capitalism. Third, we sketched and provided several examples of the base/superstructure concept which, in Marxist theory, suggests how class-based divisions influence – though they do not determine – the character of social, cultural, and political relations that pertain under contemporary capitalism. Fourth, and last, we reviewed Marx's theory of crisis. Again, this is a theory that stresses tendencies rather than determinations: Marx believed that capitalism is a system inclined, by its very structure, to cyclical crises. But whether or not socialism would emerge from one or another capitalist crisis was, to Marx, an open question dependent on the extent of organized worker opposition to it, and upon whether workers had developed the capacity and a will for self-governance.

Just as the development of feminisms rendered conceptions of gender more complex, and just as challenges on the basis of gender and class rendered conceptions of race analogously more complicated, so we might say that Weber sought to "complexify" Marx's ideas about class in several important respects. For one thing, Weber was not nearly as convinced as Marx that socialism would bring about "the withering away of the state." Rather, key to Weber's thinking about the contemporary world was his conviction that modern mass societies had to be organized around the bureaucratic form if they were to function efficiently. Yet, Weber believed bureaucracies were at one and the same time efficient and alienating, a position that led him to envision no exit from the "iron cage" of encroaching industrialism. For, even in the kind of democratically socialist societies Marx envisioned, bureaucracies would be necessary and unavoidable. For this reason, one might say he pointed out a kind of "reductionist" pitfall that is quite different from the ones diagnosed by Omi and Winant: as Weber saw it, Marx tended to reduce the problems of modernity (including, obviously, the problem of bureaucracies' sway) to a function of capitalism's ills.

Then, too, Weber took exception to Marx's concept of religion as the "opiate of the masses," suggesting in *The Protestant Ethic and the Spirit of*

Capitalism that capitalism itself might have originated in the West because of a decidedly cultural ethos: Calvinists' determination to reduce their anxieties about death by working hard, and not spending their profits, in ways that facilitated capitalist accumulation and capitalism's development. In this way, Weber opened the theoretical door for according culture far more independence in its effects on class and economic formation – an opening that led more contemporary class theorists, like Pierre Bourdieu, to "complexify" Marx in other ways. As we discussed in chapter 4, Bourdieu's notions of cultural capital and habitus have become increasingly familiar among sociologists and other social scientists. Rather than limiting the notion of "capital" to the economic kind focused upon by Marx, Bourdieu showed, in great detail, precisely how French society was divided by "distinctions" in tastes (for fashion, music, food, art) that are as significant as other forms of capital for understanding how capitalism reproduces itself. Another important example of "complexifying" Marx's work by incorporating the emphasis on culture found in Weber (and later in Bourdieu) is found in Stanley Aronowitz's *How Class Works*.[1] Aronowitz argues that even Bourdieu, open as he was to taking the so-called "cultural turn" seriously, nonetheless tended to explain the reproduction of class relationships more than he pointed a way toward overcoming them. Alternatively, Aronowitz calls for understanding contemporary class formation in terms of power and the prioritizing of "time over space"; Aronowitz's hope is that contemporary class theory will stir, rather than in any subtle way limit, our sense of possibilities that still exist for change. In other words, for Aronowitz (as was true for Bourdieu and other contemporary class theorists), class still very much "matters."

By Way of Pragmatic Implications

Once these traditions of studying gender, race, and class have been reviewed, then what? Should we necessarily surmise that in all cases gender, race, and class must each be taken into account everywhere that sociological and political studies are undertaken? We would argue that forced application of gender, race, and class perspectives to all studies of the social world can lead to overly mechanical academic analyses, just as one-dimensional perspectives can be too simplistic and sometimes mechanical as well. On the other hand, what we wish to suggest in concluding this volume, and in proceeding to the second task of this chapter, is that studying gender, race, and class should heighten self-reflexive sociological awareness in at least three respects.

The first point is a pragmatic one. When undertaking social research and investigations of myriad kinds, a certain amount of methodological flexibility is called for according to the character of a particular project. Here, following Robert Alford's suggestion in *The Craft of Inquiry*, we would advocate moving beyond false distinctions between "theory" and "method." Secondly, while studying gender, race, and/or class in close detail is certainly valid, so are investigations into whether common aspects of discrimination exist within these and across other kinds of human prejudices.[2] In other words, both differences between and commonalities across the study of gender, race, and class factors need to be explored. The third point returns to still another practical implication of this book: how one studies gender, race, and class in combination also matters. Assuming that writers are indeed attempting to capture the complexity of the social world through synthetic approaches and studies, problems of reductionism, as we have shown, need to be taken seriously. Analytic tensions between these dimensions have to be maintained at the same time connections and relationships are given their due. We will elaborate on each of these points in turn.

I

Some studies by their character call for emphasizing gender more than race, race more than class, or class more than gender. A number of reasons can be cited that may, from time to time, justify such relatively one-sided emphases:

(a) Methodological considerations may sometimes require stressing one dimension more than others. An interesting example of this was cited in chapter 4 when discussing Barbara Ehrenreich's *Nickel and Dimed*.[3] Ehrenreich purposely traveled to locales where the workforce was predominantly white in order to do her research. One motivation for so doing was very simple: given the close extent to which racial and class discriminations often interact, she might not have been hired as a white women were she competing with minorities; in other words, her research might not have been possible. But a secondary methodological motivation also seems valid, namely, that by holding race constant so as to focus on white workers, her results obviously bear cross-racial applicability for a wide range of American workers. No one reading *Nickel and Dimed* can come to the spurious conclusion that only minority workers are affected by jobs that are often low paid and offer scant and inadequate levels of benefits. For this reason, there are pros as well as cons to the relatively one-dimensional focus of Ehrenreich's study.

(b) Some studies focus on one dimension more than others because an author is trying to elaborate upon arguments mostly relevant to the substantive character of gender, or racism, or class as relatively separable forms of discrimination. For example, in my own book *Reconcilable Differences: Confronting Beauty, Pornography, and the Future of Feminism*, I argued that among feminists, a persistent divide recurred through the 1970s and 1980s over five "sex debates." These debates were all gender-related: pornography, prostitution (or sex work), sadomasochism, beauty, and violence against women. On each substantive topic, some feminists took positions that stressed women's individual freedoms and sexual agency (writers well known on this side of the debate were, among others, Ellen Willis and Carol Vance); other feminists took positions that emphasized the structural constraints that women experience within male-dominated societies that are still severely patriarchal in their character (writers well known on this side of the debate were, among others, Andrea Dworkin and Catherine MacKinnon). The result was a structure versus agency debate within feminist theory that is analogous to similar debates that have occurred in social theory more broadly.[4]

For each of these issues, I sought to suggest positions that would not further divide feminists but might be synthetic in terms of their positions about gender. With this in mind, I drew on common points between the two groups of feminists in terms of their positions about gender. For example, regarding cosmetic surgery, some feminists (on the agency side of this debate) think that changing one's appearance may empower women; others (on the structure side of this debate) feel that cosmetic surgery reinforces a system of sexist expectations that needs to be defied. Rather than thinking of these positions in either/or terms, though, I suggested that a more productive approach might be to move attention away from blaming women for either position they hold (so that a woman who undertakes cosmetic surgery is not made to feel guilty for her actions and is viewed compassionately). Simultaneously, though, media images that reproduce sexist beauty expectations – that women look young, slim, and, to the extent that racism has figured here as well, light-skinned rather than dark-skinned – need to be transformed so that women are not pressured to conform to beauty models.

Since beauty expectations have historically accompanied the kinds of gender divisions that were discussed in chapter 2, an analysis like the one above clearly centers on this kind of discrimination more than others. On the other hand, as I tried to show in *Reconcilable Differences*, class affects beauty expectations in various ways: for instance, whether women can afford cosmetic surgery is affected by economic situation; then, too, the very character of cultural standards of beauty can vary greatly according to class strata. Also, certain cosmetic procedures like eye operations aimed at making Asian women look more like Caucasian women presume racial biases and evaluations. Still, overall, *Reconcilable Differences* elaborated on feminist arguments developed primarily if not exclusively in the realm of gender.

An analogous example is the work of Stanley Aronowitz and William DiFazio on class. In their book *The Jobless Future*, Aronowitz and DiFazio refer to racial and gendered differences in how people are affected by technological changes that they posit have steadily been destroying jobs.[5] Yet, for substantive reasons, their argument is primarily focused on class. For Aronowitz and DiFazio argue that a long-term effect of late capitalist development is, as Marx initially predicted, to render more and more jobs obsolete. Computers replace a wide range of jobs (from, say, telephone operators to architectural draftsmen to factory line workers displaced by robotification). This means positively, on the one hand, that human beings can be freed to do increasingly meaningful and self-chosen work and, on the other, that there is an increasingly jobless future. Consequently, as Aronowitz and DiFazio recommend, changes have to be made both in the character of work as we know it and the kinds of benefits that become socially available to workers. One suggestion they make is that job hours become more flexible so that workers share jobs and benefit from an increasing amount of freed-up time. Another is that guaranteed income and a range of other benefits be made available to workers who may, from time to time and on a more structurally predictable basis, find themselves out of work. Clearly, then, these writers' analysis is one that elaborates on the contemporary character of class relationships and economic developments more than it involves gender and race per se.

(c) A third situation where it seems reasonable to pay more analytic attention to one social dimension than others is when showing, for intellectual and/or policy-related reasons, why more attention is needed in one area than another. In other words, concrete policy ramifications may ensue, and political decisions called for, depending on which factor is (or needs to be) emphasized. Thus, in previous chapters we discussed the race versus class debates that have compelled some social scientists to study a single dimension not only because of intellectual interest but because different policy decisions are intricately linked to each side. For example, if one agrees with William Julius Wilson that class has become more important than race in determining African Americans' life chances, this belief may lead to writing papers and articles that show how economic inequalities are perpetuating poverty, poor education, and inadequate health care. On the other hand, if one believes (as Stephen Steinberg did, disagreeing with Wilson, in a series of essays he wrote for the journal *New Politics*), that the depth of racial discrimination underlies disproportionately experienced economic inequalities, then one may endeavor to emphasize race. For Massey and Denton, whose book *American Apartheid* demonstrated the key role of racism in the almost impervious system of housing segregation that undergirds other forms of class-based inequities, changing housing discrimination may be the most important policy intervention.[6] Moreover, the attitude one takes toward affirmative action – whether to continue emphasizing race or gender, or as some have argued, whether to introduce class-based affirmative action – is a policy stance informed by the social dimension, race or gender or class, one believes is most important in a given situation.

That some studies call for emphasizing gender more than race, or class more than gender, means that flexibility rather than rigidity in appraising different projects is an important lesson to draw from this condensed volume and the course on "Gender, Race, and Class" which it summarizes.

II

A second implication of this book also requires elaboration. This point concerns distinguishing between situations that call for focusing theoretically on what is unique and particular about a given form of social discrimination, and those that lend themselves to investigating possibly common motivations for discriminatory feelings in general. Sometimes, as in the three examples presented above, the *cultural specificity* of one factor more than others seems most relevant for better understanding a particular social phenomenon. Other research projects, though, call attention to the possible applicability of more wide-reaching, even universalistic arguments, on the basis of mechanisms and dynamics that observers note to be recurring from one social setting (and type of discrimination) to others. More than this, even: in many cases, both particular and general social patterns mark the issues and problems that social scientists wish to study; in such instances, synthetic approaches to "Gender, Race, and Class" are indeed likely to reward the researcher and writer.

Sometimes, then, it makes sense to inquire into both (specifically) how and (generally) why people come to engage in sexist, racial, and/or class-based forms of discrimination. As suggested in the book *Sadomasochism in Everyday Life*, which indeed proposes a wide-ranging and general argument, we can sometimes view oppressive relations between genders, races, and classes as instances of dominant and subordinate relationships that are motivated by desires for power (and sometimes for powerlessness) that operate for reasons at once social and psychic in character. By this analysis, sadism and masochism exist in relation to one another as different sides of the same coin. As I argued in *Sadomasochism in Everyday Life*, sadomasochism can be defined in both psychic and social situations. What I called "sadomasochistic dynamics" can be said to be present, at individual and/or group levels, when the following conditions are met: (a) a hierarchical relationship between sadist and masochist is present, one that attributes inferiority to the latter and alleged superiority to the former; (b) mutual dependency exists for both parties, though this is actually acknowledged only by the masochist; and (c) the presence of a sadomasochistic dynamic can be judged by a set of reprisals (consequences of some kind are bound to ensue) that unfold if the masochist attempts to challenge, rebel from, or otherwise break a bond that exists with the sadist.[7]

In other words, a sadist can be said to be a party who wishes to experience greater certainty in life (and therefore greater power) by hindering the freedom of another. Even though he or she actually depends, symbiotically, on the masochist (for how can one even conceive of a "sadistic" party unless there is a "masochistic" one?), the sadist acts as though he or she were independent and utterly in control. On the other hand, a masochist is a party whose sense of certainty may be increased by subordinating herself or himself to another. Even though she or he is actually more independent than may appear, the masochist acts as though she or he is dependent and out of control (indeed, she or he may have initially been placed through social circumstances, originally quite involuntarily, in precisely this position). What I contend in *Sadomasochism in Everyday Life*, though, is that this dynamic between the sadist and masochist, masochist and sadist, is necessarily dynamic and constantly in flux. Thus, over time, sadomasochistic dynamics have a tendency to generate cyclical "crises" in a way that is analogous – in a wide range of psychic as well as social, individual as well as collective, settings – to the kinds of economic "crises" Marxist theory more narrowly predicts.

Consequently, *Sadomasochism in Everyday Life* exemplifies one mode of analysis that can be applied across the board to some gendered relationships (say, between a batterer and his/her victim), to some racialized relationships (say, the relations between black employees and white employers in many situations under previously existing South African apartheid), and certainly to some class-stratified relationships (say, between a sadistic employer and a masochistically situated employee). At the same time, a last overriding and defining criterion of sadomasochism is its transformability: a sadist has the constant potential of becoming a masochist, and vice versa. Applied to a hierarchically structured social world, this is where the A/B/C diagram mentioned in previous chapters comes into play. For someone who is situated in a relatively powerful position in one sphere of her life (say, a white woman who employs a woman of color as a domestic) may be relatively powerless in another (say, in relation to her white male husband). Sadomasochistic dynamics can therefore appear within gender, race, or class relationships of power or between them.

Moreover, going back yet once more to the conceptual vocabulary introduced in chapter 1, nothing about who occupies which position in a sadomasochistic dynamic is essentially – or essentialistically – determined or fixed. Sadists can be men or women, masochists women or men; within each position can conceivably be found parties of diverse races, classes, or sexual orientations. But wherever they appear, what is suggested here is that an underlying motivation may be the same across each of these otherwise quite different dimensions of social life. For the batterer in a gendered relationship, the discriminating party in a racialized relationship, and a particularly sadistic boss in a class relationship may, each in her or his own way, be seeking what Frankfurt School theorist Erich Fromm referred to as escapes from existential anxieties and insecurities born of freedom.[8] To oppress or discriminate against someone else seeks to ensure that the other person, as a result, has fewer options and remains tied to the discriminating party. As a result, this discriminating party appears to be "more free" due to the certainty another's subordination has secured. As classic sociological theorist Emile Durkheim also understood well, social policies and systems (whether capitalistic or authoritarian) can aggravate or alleviate such sadistic desires for power – whether desires for gender, racialized, or class-related powers – by the extent to which they provide, or fail to provide, offsetting social securities in the broadest sense.

But *Sadomasochism in Everyday Life* is only one example of an argument that envisions not only differences but commonalities – and therefore has a "universalistic" aspect – in how and why gender, racial, and class discriminations operate. Other perspectives have also gone in the direction of making broadly general arguments about how psychology and the social interconnect. Not only Erich Fromm but other writings in the Frankfurt School tradition have had this orientation. Much more recently, political scientist Joseph Schwartz has also insisted on the importance of not losing a sense of commonalities and universals at the same time as theorists maintain a more precise understanding of how gender, race, and class are specific and distinctive dimensions of the social world.

III

A third "lesson" of this volume follows. Throughout the previous chapters, we have repeatedly criticized reductionist perspectives on the social world – ones that declare gender discrimination, or racial discrimination, or class discrimination, to be at fault – on the basis of their over-simplicity. Often, a preferable if challenging option to approaching the many social settings wherein gender, race, and class and other discriminations obviously overlap is to maintain an analytic tension between the autonomy and the interrelatedness of each. For intellectual, political, and policy benefits do accrue from thinking synthetically about gender, race, and class – that is, from according each of these dimensions its due at the same time as we take care not to reduce one dimension to any other.

Here, then, is the crux of this short volume's overall argument in favor of "complexifying" social analyses about gender, race, class, and other social discriminations as a matter of course. From the late 1980s (when we started teaching this course) until now, awareness of "intersectionality" has already transformed many academic disciplines. It is far more common now than before to find scholars in the humanities and in diverse social sciences almost routinely discussing gender aspects of a project that primarily concerns problems stemming from class, or class aspects of a project that primarily concerns problems stemming from racism. Still, this may happen in courses on race, or class, or gender within sociology, political science, or anthropology departments: in other words, an integrative focus has not necessarily become the subject matter of many courses per se.

Consequently, at this concluding juncture, it may make sense to provide examples of two quite different attempts at incorporating all three dimensions – gender, race, and class – into scholarly work that deals with problems wherein all three kinds of social discriminations became overtly enmeshed. What are the advantages of so doing? Both of the instances about to be discussed involved efforts to maintain the kind of analytic tension alluded to above, and to avoid reductionism. However the way in which gender, race, and class were incorporated, more specifically, varies from one instance to the other, illustrating the myriad ways that such syntheses can take place. First, a prime illustration of literally incorporating co-considerations of class, race, and gender into an ethnographic study is found in anthropologist Philippe Bourgois's award-winning text *In Search of Respect: Selling Crack in El Barrio*.[9] Another way of incorporating these dimensions, while keeping a sense of tension between them, entails looking at how these different discriminations were responded to not only by individuals but also by social movements. Secondly, then, we focus on a book that examined reactions to crime cases in the 1980s and 1990s, including social movement reactions which were played against each other divisively. This book, entitled *High Profile Crimes: When Legal Cases Become Social Causes*, was also written by one of this volume's authors.

Bourgois's In Search of Respect

Bourgois's *In Search of Respect* is a study of male drug dealers, largely Puerto Rican, in El Barrio (East Harlem) in New York City. In the introduction to the book, Bourgois immediately places El Barrio in a larger context of other New York City neighborhoods: he provides a map to aid in visualization, as well as ample statistics that testify to nearly half the families in the area falling below the US poverty line, and requiring food stamps just to get by. Thus, Bourgois instantly provides a sense of the social structure, in class terms, of his subject matter. But he also entitles the very next chapter "Violating Apartheid in the United States" – a reference, like the title of *American Apartheid*, that calls the reader's attention to the racial segregation characterizing this country at the local level. In this chapter, Bourgois demonstrates how closely racism and class discrimination have interacted in the lives of the young men – Primo, Cesar, Ray – whom he befriends in El Barrio. Yet, they are not the same. Attesting to their interrelationship is that the vast majority of people who live in El Barrio are both minority and working-class or poor. Bourgois, on the other hand, both comes from a relatively well-to-do background and is white. Indeed, to see a white face, like Bourgois's, is to risk being thought (as Bourgois, who is called "Felipe," is initially thought to be by his drug-dealing friends) a "cop" and to have police, on the other hand, think he buys drugs. (Why else would he be in the neighborhood, it is wondered?) However, race and class are separable in other circumstances. In fact, most poor families in the US are white (in absolute numbers) even as a disproportionate percentage of poor families (relatively speaking) are members of minority groups.

In Search of Respect also relates Felipe's friends' encounters with racial discrimination through their less than ideal educational experiences. Felipe unwittingly "disrespects" Ray in front of the other young men by reading a newspaper article out loud which mentions his own research. What Felipe does not realize, though, is that Ray cannot read, having not been properly educated in American schools. His other friends also recount, in a chapter on "School Days," a lack of sensitivity toward Spanish-speaking children in the educational system that translates into feelings of exclusion and denigration for both them and their parents. As Bourgois describes the experience of a young man named Primo:

> In his kindergarten homeroom, Primo inherited the instantaneous onus of his mother's identity as a former rural plantation worker, and now new-immigrant inner-city sweatshop employee. Her functional illiteracy and her inability to communicate with the educational bureaucracy condemned Primo to appear uncooperative and slow-witted to his teachers...it is in school that the full force of middle-class society's definitions of appropriate cultural capital and symbolic violence comes crashing down on a working-class Puerto Rican child. (pp. 176–7)

Note that Bourgois is treating class and race discrimination to some extent as interwoven pieces of day-to-day experiences. Clearly, his mother's class position has also affected how he is treated; notice, too, that Bourgois makes direct reference, here and in other places throughout *In Search of Respect*, to Bourdieu's expansive notion (see chapter 4) of cultural capital. On the other hand, though, some sort of tension has been maintained here between the two dimensions insofar as class and race are not being reduced to one another. A white working-class child might also suffer from symbolic violence and "inappropriate" cultural capital. But being Spanish-speaking and Puerto Rican is also a socially specific experience that seems to compound the levels of discrimination Primo encounters.

If class and race are treated at once separably and together, though, what about gender – where does this fit into Bourgois's richly textured ethnographic account? At the time of his research, Bourgois was well aware of the increased attention social scientists had been paying to gender since the movements of the 1960s and 1970s. As a white male ethnographer, he makes clear his desire to describe the workings of gender as well as race and class. An interesting question we have often asked students at Barnard, Columbia, and Fordham, though, is whether Bourgois succeeds. One fascinatingly controversial aspect of *In Search of Respect* suggests that he does; Bourgois relates how, after getting to know Primo, Ray, Cesar, and others so intimately, they eventually felt comfortable enough with him to recount a gang rape in which the young men had participated years earlier. Indeed, in telling "Felipe" what happened, there is initially little sense of shame or guilt, as though gang rape were just another experience to be shared with another man. Bourgois describes his dilemma when faced with this disclosure. On the one hand, an important goal of his study is to humanize a group of people – of drug dealers – whose backgrounds and problems (of class and race discrimination) have been largely overlooked, and labeled as deviant, by mainstream society. On the other hand, could Bourgois simply ignore the fact that rape comprises yet another form of discrimination, and is an act that he as a writer/scholar himself condemned? In the interest of veracity, Bourgois did evidently decide to describe the rape, and its recounting to him by a young woman, even if in so doing he potentially reinforced rather than diluted already existing social stigmatization.

Thus, through this act of rape, gender bias is introduced in a way that clearly differentiates it from other forms of discrimination, that is, race and class prejudices. Simultaneously, the A/B/C diagram this book has suggested can be useful in illustrating that the transformability of a sadomasochistic dynamics can help analytically to understand the young men's multi-dimensioned experiences. The experience of social marginalization in class and race terms (as just described), and the sexual objectification and violence enacted against a young woman seem to displace powerlessness and transform it into power. Another way of putting this is that to the extent that the young men were situated masochistically in terms of their class and race position, they still could exert power sadistically in terms of their gender-based position. As described in chapter 3, too, R. W. Connell's categories of marginalized masculinity also apply here in that even though these young men (in class and race terms) cannot partake of the dominant hegemonic masculinity, a certain degree of compensatory power was possible through acts and practices that subordinated women.[10]

In these respects, then, Bourgois does seem to succeed at integrating simultaneous awareness of class, race, and gender biases into his study while avoiding reductionism that would deny the relatively autonomous aspects of each. But a case can also be made, and has been made by students over the years who have debated the pros and cons of Bourgois's synthetic efforts, arguing that of the three social dimensions gender is the most shortchanged by *In Search of Respect*. For one thing, Bourgois's study focuses far less on women's experiences than on men's. One woman, named Candy, whom Ray knew and worked with, is described at some length but only because she was the most involved with the drug business. Other women's voices – girlfriends, daughters, and mothers, parties who just were around the neighborhood – are barely heard. One obvious explanation for this is that, had Bourgois gone down this route, he might have been viewed more suspiciously by Primo, Ray, Cesar, and his other friends: was he "hitting" on their girlfriends, they might have wondered? Was he trustworthy? For one can certainly argue that, given Bourgois's own upper-class background and relative immunity from racism, the most important source of his ability to "bond" with the young men he befriended was on the basis of a commonly shared masculinity. Had he gotten to know more women in the neighborhood, this commonality might have been threatened. Yet some students made reasonable arguments, in discussing this synthetic attempt at length, whether more could have been done. Perhaps Bourgois could have incorporated his wife's experiences with other women since she, too, moved into El Barrio with him in order to work on this study. Perhaps graduate students or other academic colleagues of Bourgois's who are women could have done additional research as part of his own project.

To the extent that these arguments are convincing, they suggest that the depth of awareness to class and race discriminations evinced by *In Search of Respect* is not entirely matched by its probing of gender, and the effect of gender on young lower-class Puerto Rican men's lives. But to the extent that this was not the express intention of Bourgois's work, and that greater incorporation of gender-related data from women's point of view was not possible, the study stands as a valiant effort to exemplify the kind of complexity we have been discussing throughout this work on gender, race, and class.

Chancer's High-Profile Crimes[11]

Another example of probing relationships between gender, race, and class discriminations, in a way that hopefully also does not reduce consideration of one dimension to a function of the other, takes us into the realm of reactions to high-profile US crime cases of the 1980s and 1990s. This study looked at a particular subgroup of all high-profile crimes which drew intensive media and public attention from the time of the Central Park jogger case (a rape committed in New York City in 1989), through the O. J. Simpson case (a double homicide of which Simpson stood accused in 1994, and was convicted of having committed in 1995).

The book's overall thesis is that, through these decades, high-profile crime cases of the kind that Chancer dubs "provoking assaults" became a way of negotiating, arguing about, and trying to absorb issues of gender, race, and class discrimination that social movements of the 1960s had brought to conscious awareness – including, but not limited to, precisely the kind of issues discussed in this book. Violent crimes that received high-profile media attention during these decades reflected a historical conjuncture of three different circumstances: (a) the issue of crime, especially violent crime, was increasingly worrying Americans; (b) social movements about gender, race, and class discrimination in the US had moved onto the defensive (especially after a creeping conservatism slowly began around 1980, which was only slightly relieved during the Clinton years), so that violent crimes of concern to the public was a good "consciousness-raising" vehicle for bias-related issues; and (c) the mass media had become more competitive, both within the newspaper business and between newspapers and other outlets such as television, cable, and internet news, creating an "infrastructure" distinctively capable of publicizing crimes and debates over crimes, writ large.

Once these historical circumstances came to overlap, violent crimes that were symbolic of discrimination – particularly gender- and race-based discriminations – became the most high-profile crimes of the 1980s and 1990s. Racially oriented cases surfaced in the form of the famous New York City Howard Beach and Bensonhurst cases, both centered on young black men who had been murdered essentially because of the color of their skin; later, in Los Angeles, police brutality was vividly symbolized by the notorious Rodney King case. In the realm of gender, the Central Park jogger case involved the brutal rape of a young white investment banker in 1989, while the William Kennedy Smith and Mike Tyson cases of 1991–2 again brought debates about rape to broad public awareness.

But the use of high-profile crime cases to symbolize issues of racial and gender-based discrimination in America was complicated – involving, from the public's point of view, both advantages and disadvantages – insofar as the following argument can be made. Gender and racial discrimination, as we saw in chapters 2 and 3, are multi-dimensional in their social causation (illustrating, through prior instances, the pitfalls of reductionism). Yet, to the extent these social problems came to be symbolized through high-profile crime cases, an only two-sided legal structure (in which one side comes to represent the prosecution and the other side the defense) was superimposed on issues far more complex than this structure could bear. Legal cases result, as they should, in verdicts; say, either William Kennedy Smith did or did not rape the woman who accused him of the crime. Yet, once individual legal cases become confused with social causes, an acquittal for Smith (precisely what happened) may be taken as a symbolic "loss" insofar as this individual legal case was taken to provide an indicator of how seriously violence against women overall was being treated in the US.

Moreover, what complicates matters further is that in many of the cases investigated in *High-Profile Crimes*, one dimension of social discrimination came to be played against another. In the Central Park jogger case, the prosecution side became symbolically associated with the cause of women's freedom to be able to jog wherever and whenever they pleased. But the defense side also had an important concern, namely, were a group of minority men being stigmatized by the mass media as traveling in "wolf packs" and allegedly engaging in "wilding" to such a degree that a fair trial became especially hard to procure? Because of the either/or, win/lose legal structure in which individual crime cases necessarily play out, only one side could win.

The same held true for the O. J. Simpson case wherein, once more, two social movement issues – one involving gender bias and the other racism – became counterposed against one another. On the prosecution's side, this time the symbolized feminist issue was domestic violence; on the defense's side, the racially loaded issue of police brutality and misconduct in post-Rodney King Los Angeles became contentious. Indeed, what Chancer has elsewhere dubbed a long pattern of "playing gender against race" has meant that black males through the 1980s became well-known symbols of feminist issues. In 1991, Mike Tyson became arguably the most well-known symbol of rape in American history to date; in 1992, Clarence Thomas became arguably the most well-known symbol of sexual harassment in American history to date; and, in 1995, O. J. Simpson became arguably the most well-known symbolic representative of domestic violence to date. In each of these instances, race was played against gender: it was hard to wish for an outcome in which both these forms of discrimination could be recognized and redressed within the two-sided structure of cases that became allied with causes.

What about class in all this? Interestingly, as this book draws to a close, yet another observation comes full circle. Just as in years of teaching "Gender, Race, and Class" students often seemed to relate more easily to gender and racial discrimination than to class – a situation partly explicable in terms of the US left having been relatively powerless in comparison to other advanced industrial countries in, say, Western Europe, Eastern Europe, and Scandinavia – so these cases foregrounded race and gender in American cultural discourse more than class. Yet, certainly, class was present in these cases just as it continues to play an influential role, broadly speaking, in US culture and politics: a fascinating contrast in cultural capital differentiates the situation of the Central Park young minority defendants (who could barely afford good lawyers to represent them and who were, in some cases, not very well represented) from that of O. J. Simpson (who was able to hire a "dream team" of lawyers to defend him, with obviously an effective result).

Thus, all three social dimensions – gender, race, and class – were clearly involved in the Central Park jogger and O. J. Simpson cases. But this example also illustrates how, under certain circumstances, the role of one or two of these factors may be quite visible while others stay relatively hidden. In Bourgois's ethnography *In Search of Respect*, it was the place of gender that the author needed self-consciously to delve into, to uncover. In high-profile crimes from the Central Park jogger case to the O. J. Simpson case, I found that attention to gender and racial discrimination (albeit in opposition to one another) was much more apparent in public discourse than attention to class; it was the latter dimension, by contrast, that needed highlighting.

And, Again, in Sum

But, with this, we find ourselves wondering about how social movements, at present, can themselves best interrelate. One legacy of the 1960s and 1970s was the approach to organizing that has often been called "identity politics"; this presumed that people joined social movements (for example, the civil rights, feminist, or gay rights movements) on the basis of discrimination that they were directly experiencing on the grounds of their expressed sexual preferences or physical characteristics (for example, racial or gendered traits). Consequently, this basis for organizing focuses on people's commonalities within categories that vary from one social movement's emphasis to another's. On the other hand, the influence of poststructuralist and postmodern orientations decades later, though dating back to the 1980s and 1990s, has resulted in serious criticisms of identity politics. Questioning whether identity itself is an essentialistic notion – whether the particular identity in question was one's race, one's gender, or even one's sexuality (as queer theorists, in this vein, have wondered) – has inspired poststructuralists from Foucault to Butler to lay a theoretical ground for political organizing that also often takes place on the basis of complex coalitions and overlapping affiliations. Within such coalitions, it would not be unusual to find a man who is white, gay, and a corporate manager marching against the war in Iraq or for reproductive choice with, say, a straight Latina working-class woman

– a political alliance that evokes the simultaneous reality that, in huge numbers of cases, differences exist alongside equally noteworthy commonalities. A sense of greater complexity, then, has tended to grow and to prevail in how most groups approach questions of gender, racial, class-based, and other forms of discrimination in and outside the classroom.

Indeed, in closing, these reflections raise the question of how courses like "Gender, Race, and Class" relate to the larger world wherein debates and issues about these frequently overlapping brands of discrimination still rage, and are experienced and thought about as anything but abstract. I used to begin "Gender, Race, and Class" by telling students that, whatever else the course stimulated in them, they would not leave the classroom feeling that what they had read, seen, heard, and heatedly argued with each other about had nothing to do with the so-called "real world" outside academe. This was and is a beauty of sociology in general, and of "Gender, Race, and Class" in particular. We wanted students to start to think differently about the news, to connect debates over gender, race, and class – separately and in combination – with concerns as to whether reproductive rights were going to stay legalized, with reflection on whether or not race and class were both being given adequate attention when stories came up that had to do with, say, poverty, residential housing segregation, or the diminishing (or, in the US, the elimination) of welfare benefits. And we wanted them to question, among so many other critical queries, how gender fits into all this for both men and women.

By the end of the course, though, we hoped all this would be more than academic in yet another way. For obviously, with this as with the history of so many other courses of study, subject matters offered in departments of universities cannot be fully separated from the social context which gave birth to them and which continually evolves. So, too, our hopes as teachers was that generations of students would try to alter the complicated world they were studying for the better – inside but also out, beyond, the room in which we had been sitting. Perhaps they would conclude, as did Matty Rich's poignant film *Straight Out of Brooklyn* – itself a very non-academic model of incorporating class, race, and gender – that "we have to change." However multi-dimensional and analytically challenging "Gender, Race, and Class" is at the moment, and is likely to be for many years and even decades to come, still – one hopes, ironically enough – that the basis for studying it may one day become irrelevant.

Notes

I Why Gender, Race, and Class?

1 Margaret L. Andersen and Patricia Hill Collins (comps.), *Race, Class and Gender: An Anthology*, 3rd edn., Belmont, Calif.: Wadsworth, 1998.

2 C. Wright Mills, *The Sociological Imagination*, New York: Oxford University Press, 2000.

3 Peter L. Berger and Thomas Luckmann, *The Social Construction of Reality: A Treatise in the Sociology of Knowledge*, Garden City, NY: Doubleday, 1966; John Berger, *Ways of Seeing*, London and New York: BBC/Penguin Books, 1991.

4 Richard J. Herrnstein and Charles A. Murray, *The Bell Curve: Intelligence and Class Structure in American Life*, New York: Free Press, 1994.

5 Claude S. Fischer et al., *Inequality by Design: Cracking the Bell Curve Myth*, Princeton: Princeton University Press, 1996.

6 Shulamith Firestone, *The Dialectic of Sex: The Case for Feminist Revolution*, London: Women's Press, 1979.

7 William Julius Wilson, *The Declining Significance of Race: Blacks and Changing American Institutions*, 2nd edn., Chicago: University of Chicago Press, 1980; William Julius Wilson, *The Truly Disadvantaged: The Inner City, the Underclass, and Public Policy*, Chicago: University of Chicago Press, 1987; William Julius Wilson, *When Work Disappears: The World of the New Urban Poor*, New York: Alfred A. Knopf, distr. by Random House, 1996.

8 Judith Butler, *Gender Trouble: Feminism and the Subversion of Identity*, New York: Routledge, 1990.

9 Konrad Lorenz, *On Aggression*, New York: Bantam Books, 1966.

10 Sigmund Freud, *Civilization and Its Discontents*, New York: W. W. Norton, 1989.

11 Emile Durkheim, *The Rules of Sociological Method, and Selected Texts on Sociology and Its Method*, ed. Steven Lukes, London: Macmillan, 1982.

12 Stanley Cohen, *Folk Devils and Moral Panics: The Creation of the Mods and Rockers*, Oxford: Blackwell, 1987.

13 Jack Katz, *Seductions of Crime: Moral and Sensual Attractions in Doing Evil*, New York: Basic Books, 1988.

14 Lynn Chancer, *Sadomasochism in Everyday Life: The Dynamics of Power and Powerlessness*, New Brunswick, NJ: Rutgers University Press, 1992.

2 Gender Defined and Refined

1 See Simone de Beauvoir, *The Second Sex*, New York: Vintage Books, 1974, in particular the chapters entitled "The Facts of Biology" and "Childhood."

2 This exercise is done each year in Chancer's "Gender, Race, and Class" course. Students consistently blurt out the aforementioned terms. The interpretation of gender flows from Emile Durkheim's concept of "social facts" – aspects or characteristics of social life that the individual finds at birth; the meanings ascribed to, for example, gender or race, are not of the individual's own choosing but possess immeasurable strength because people have become accustomed to them. Durkheim argues that "social facts" are resistant, almost impervious to change. Moreover, in the process of changing social facts a new set is created. See Emile Durkheim et al., *The Rules of Sociological Method*, 8th edn., Glencoe, Ill.: Free Press, 1950

3 Edwin McCarthy Lemert, *Human Deviance, Social Problems, and Social Control*, Englewood Cliffs, NJ: Prentice-Hall, 1967.

4 Simone de Beauvoir, *The Second Sex*, New York: Vintage Books, 1974. Judith Butler, *Gender Trouble: Feminism and the Subversion of Identity*, Thinking Gender, New York: Routledge, 1990.

5 As she writes: "But the boys especially are little by little denied the kisses and caresses they have been used to. As for the little girl, she continues to be cajoled, she is allowed to cling to her mother's skirts, her father takes her on his knee strokes her hair . . . bodily contacts and agreeable glances protect her against the anguish of solitude. The little boy, in contrast, will be denied even coquetry: his efforts at enticement, his play-acting, are irritating. He is told that 'a man doesn't look at himself in the mirror . . . a man doesn't cry.' He is urged to be a 'little man'" (de Beauvoir, *The Second Sex*, p. 305).

6 For psychoanalytic discussions of gender socialization see: Nancy Chodorow, *The Reproduction of Mothering: Psychoanalysis and the Sociology of Gender*, Berkeley: University of California Press, 1978; Jessica Benjamin, *The Bonds of Love: Psychoanalysis, Feminism, and the Problem of Domination*, New York: Pantheon Books, 1988; Margaret S. Mahler, Anni Bergman, and Mahler Research Foundation, *The Psychological Birth of the Human Infant: The Separation-Individuation Process*, videorecording, Mahler Research Foundation, Franklin Lakes, NJ, 1983.

7 See Ruth Milkman, *Gender at Work: The Dynamics of Job Segregation by Sex during World War II*, Urbana: University of Illinois Press, 1987; Ruth Milkman, *Women, Work, and Protest: A Century of US Women's Labor History*, Boston: Routledge & Kegan Paul, 1985.

8 See Victor R. Fuchs, *Women's Quest for Economic Equality*, Cambridge, Mass.: Harvard University Press, 1988.

9   For detailed discussion see: Evelyn Fox Keller and Helen E. Longino, *Feminism and Science*, Oxford Readings in Feminism, Oxford and New York: Oxford University Press, 1996; Sandra G. Harding, *The Science Question in Feminism*, Ithaca, NY: Cornell University Press, 1986.

10 For an analysis see: Alice Kessler-Harris, *Out to Work: A History of Wage-Earning Women in the United States*, New York: Oxford University Press, 1982; Ronnie Steinberg, Deborah M. Figart, and American Academy of Political and Social Science, *Emotional Labor in the Service Economy*, Annals of the American Academy of Political and Social Science 561, Thousand Oaks, Calif.: Sage Publications, 1999. The ways in which race is also at play here will be discussed in chapter 3. However, it is important to note that low-level workers in general, and health-care workers in particular, are disproportionately people of color whereas high-level workers such as management are disproportionately white.

11 Martha Fineman and Nancy Sweet Thomadsen, *At the Boundaries of Law: Feminism and Legal Theory*, New York: Routledge, 1991.

12 Suzanne J. Kessler and Wendy McKenna, *Gender: An Ethnomethodological Approach*, New York: Wiley, 1978, p. 7.

13 See Butler, *Gender Trouble*.

14 Candace West and Don H. Zimmerman, "Doing Gender," *Gender and Society*, 1: 2 (June 1987), pp. 125–51.

15 Sherry Ortner, "Is Female to Male as Nature is to Culture?" in Michelle Zimbalist Rosaldo and Louise Lamphere (eds.), *Women, Culture and Society*, Stanford, Calif.: Stanford University Press, 1974, pp. 67–87.

16 See introduction by Eleanor Burke Leacock, in Lewis Henry Morgan, *Ancient Society, or, Researches in the Lines of Human Progress from Savagery through Barbarism to Civilization*, Gloucester, Mass.: P. Smith, 1974.

17 Friedrich Engels, *The Origin of the Family, Private Property, and the State, in the Light of the Researches of Lewis H. Morgan*, intro. and notes by Eleanor Burke Leacock, 1st edn., New York: International Publishers, 1972.

18 Morgan and Leacock, *Ancient Society*.

19 Engels writes: "The overthrow of mother right was the world-historic defeat of the female sex. The man seized the reins in the house also, the woman was degraded, enthralled, the slave of the man's lust, a mere instrument for breeding children" (Engels, *The Origin of the Family*, p. 120).

20 Diana E. H. Russell, *Rape in Marriage*, New York: Collier Books, 1983, pp. 21–3.

21 Carole Pateman, *The Sexual Contract*, Stanford, Calif.: Stanford University Press, 1988.

22 Susan Brownmiller, *Against Our Will: Men, Women, and Rape*, New York: Simon & Schuster, 1975.

23 Ruth Schwartz Cowan, *More Work for Mother: The Ironies of Household Technology from the Open Hearth to the Microwave*, New York: Basic Books, 1983; Arlie Russell Hochschild, *The Second Shift: Working Parents and the Revolution at Home*, New York: Viking, 1989.

24 Some interesting works on this topic are: Gloria Anzaldúa, *Making Face, Making Soul/Haciendo Caras: Creative and Critical Perspectives by Women of Color*, 1st edn., San Francisco: Aunt Lute Foundation Books, 1990; Domitila Barrios de Chungara and Moema Viezzer, *Let Me Speak: Testimony of Domitila, a Woman of the Bolivian Mines*, New York: Monthly Review Press, 1978; Miroslava Chavez-Garcia, *Negotiating Conquest: Gender and Power in California, 1770s to 1880s*, Tucson: University of Arizona Press, 2004; Evelyn Nakano Glenn, *Unequal Freedom: How Race and Gender Shaped American Citizenship and Labor*, Cambridge, Mass. and London: Harvard University Press, 2002; Evelyn Nakano Glenn, *Issei, Nisei, War Bride: Three Generations of Japanese American Women in Domestic Service*, Philadelphia: Temple University Press, 1986; Maxine Hong Kingston, *The Woman Warrior: Memoirs of a Girlhood among Ghosts*, New York: Vintage Books, 1989; Maxine Hong Kingston, Luisa Valenzuela, and Stephanie Dowrick, *Two Foreign Women: Maxine Hong Kingston, Luisa Valenzuela*, Leichhardt, NSW: Pluto Press, 1990; Gayatri Chakravorty Spivak, *Thinking Academic Freedom in Gendered Post-Coloniality*, Cape Town: University of Cape Town, 1992; Gayatri Chakravorty Spivak, *In Other Worlds: Essays in Cultural Politics*, New York: Methuen, 1987; T. Minh-Ha Trinh, *When the Moon Waxes Red: Representation, Gender, and Cultural Politics*, New York: Routledge, 1991; T. Minh-Ha Trinh, *Woman, Native, Other: Writing Postcoloniality and Feminism*, Bloomington: Indiana University Press, 1989.

25 See Peggy Antrobus, *The Global Women's Movement: Origins, Issues and Strategies*, London: Zed Books, 2004, in particular chs. 6, 8, and 10.

26 John Stuart Mill, *The Subjection of Women*, ed. Susan Moller Okin, Indianapolis: Hackett, 1988.

27 Mary Wollstonecraft, *A Vindication of the Rights of Women*, Buffalo, NY: Prometheus Books, 1989.

28 Betty Friedan, *The Feminine Mystique*, New York: W. W. Norton, 1983.

29 For detailed discussion see: Jo Freeman, *The Politics of Women's Liberation: A Case Study of an Emerging Social Movement and Its Relation to the Policy Process*, New York: McKay, 1975; Judith Hole and Ellen Levine, *Rebirth of Feminism*, New York: Quadrangle Books, 1973.

30 The first proposal of the Equal Rights Amendment in the 1920s met with similar resistance. See Nancy Cott's essay, "Historical Perspectives: the Equal Rights Amendment in the 1920s," in Marianne Hirsch and Evelyn Fox Keller (eds.), *Conflicts in Feminism*, New York: Routledge, 1990.

31 For a detailed analysis see Jane J. Mansbridge, *Why We Lost the ERA*, Chicago: University of Chicago Press, 1986; Mary Frances Berry, *Why ERA Failed: Politics, Women's Rights, and the Amending Process of the Constitution*, Bloomington: Indiana University Press, 1986.

32 Phyllis Schlafly mounted a fierce campaign against the amendment, starting the National Committee to Stop ERA soon after it was submitted to the states. See Rosenberg's discussion of Schlafly's campaign in Rosalind Rosenberg,

Divided Lives: American Women in the Twentieth Century, ed. Eric Foner, New York: Hill & Wang, 1992, ch. 7.

33 For a discussion of the concept of the family wage see: Linda Gordon, *Pitied but Not Entitled: Single Mothers and the History of Welfare, 1890–1935*, New York: Free Press; Toronto: Maxwell Macmillan Canada, 1994; Claudia Dale Goldin, *Understanding the Gender Gap: An Economic History of American Women*, New York: Oxford University Press, 1990; Rosenberg, *Divided Lives*.

34 In the late twentieth century the voices of diverse groups of women began to be incorporated into American feminist discourse and texts. An analysis will follow in chapter 3.

35 Betty Friedan, *It Changed My Life: Writings on the Women's Movement*, Cambridge, Mass.: Harvard University Press, 1998.

36 Kate Millett, *Sexual Politics*, Garden City, NY: Doubleday, 1970; Shulamith Firestone, *The Dialectic of Sex: The Case for Feminist Revolution*, London: Women's Press, 1979.

37 Kristin Luker, *Abortion and the Politics of Motherhood*, California Series on Social Choice and Political Economy, Berkeley: University of California Press, 1984; Alice Echols, *Daring to Be Bad: Radical Feminism in America, 1967–1975*, Minneapolis: University of Minnesota Press, 1989.

38 Boston Women's Health Book Collective, *Our Bodies, Ourselves*, New York: Simon & Schuster, 1973.

39 Millett, *Sexual Politics*.

40 For a detailed analysis of power relations see: Lynn S. Chancer, *Sadomasochism in Everyday Life: The Dynamics of Power and Powerlessness*, New Brunswick, NJ: Rutgers University Press, 1992.

41 Sara M. Evans, *Personal Politics: The Roots of Women's Liberation in the Civil Rights Movement and the New Left*, New York: Vintage Books, 1980.

42 In the play, a group of women, led by an Athenian woman named Lysistrata withhold sex from their husbands as a protest to the war (Aristophanes, *Lysistrata*, trans. Douglass Parker, New York: Signet Classic, 2001).

43 Ti-Grace Atkinson, *Amazon Odyssey: Collection of Writings*, New York: Links Books, distr. Quick Fox, 1974.

44 See Gerda Lerner (ed.), *Black Women in White America: A Documentary History*, New York: Vintage Books, 1973.

45 See Michèle Barrett, *Women's Oppression Today: Problems in Marxist Feminist Analysis*, London: New Left Books, 1980; Rosemary Hennessy and Chrys Ingraham, *Materialist Feminism: A Reader in Class, Difference, and Women's Lives*, New York: Routledge, 1997.

46 Cowan, *More Work for Mother*; Kessler-Harris, *Out to Work*; Milkman, *Women, Work, and Protest*; Hochschild, *The Second Shift*.

47 Juliet Mitchell, *Woman's Estate*, New York: Pantheon Books, 1972; Ann Oakley, *Woman's Work: The Housewife, Past and Present*, New York: Pantheon Books, 1975; Sheila Rowbotham, *Woman's Consciousness, Man's World*, Harmondsworth: Penguin, 1973.

48 Ronnie Steinberg, *Wages and Hours: Labor and Reform in Twentieth-Century America*, New Brunswick, NJ: Rutgers University Press, 1982; Steinberg, Figart, and American Academy of Political and Social Science, *Emotional Labor in the Service Economy*.

49 For discussion see Rosenberg, *Divided Lives*, and Nancy C. M. Hartsock, *Money, Sex, and Power: Toward a Feminist Historical Materialism*, Northeastern Series in Feminist Theory, Boston: Northeastern University Press, 1985.

50 Zillah R. Eisenstein (ed.), *Capitalist Patriarchy and the Case for Socialist Feminism*, New York: Monthly Review Press, 1978.

51 For an overview of feminist theory and the issue of prostitution see Lynn S. Chancer, *Reconcilable Differences: Confronting Beauty, Pornography, and the Future of Feminism*, Berkeley: University of California Press, 1998, ch. 5. For an analysis of the patriarchal roots of prostitution see two important works on the intersection of prostitution and the exploitation of women in the drug culture: Lisa Maher, *Sexed Work: Gender, Race, and Resistance in a Brooklyn Drug Market*, Clarendon Studies in Criminology, Oxford: New York: Clarendon Press, 1997; Mitchell S. Ratner, *Crack Pipe as Pimp: An Ethnographic Investigation of Sex-for-Crack Exchanges*, New York: Lexington Books; Toronto: Maxwell Macmillan Canada, 1993.

52 Bell Hooks, *Ain't I a Woman: Black Women and Feminism*, Boston: South End Press, 1981; Bell Hooks, *Feminist Theory from Margin to Center*, Boston: South End Press, 1984; Patricia Hill Collins, *Black Feminist Thought: Knowledge, Consciousness, and the Politics of Empowerment*, Perspectives on Gender 2, Boston: Unwin Hyman, 1990; Patricia Hill Collins, *Black Sexual Politics: African Americans, Gender, and the New Racism*, New York: Routledge, 2004.

53 Hooks, *Feminist Theory from Margin to Center*, pp. 19–30; Zillah R. Eisenstein, *The Radical Future of Liberal Feminism*, Longman Series in Feminist Theory, New York: Longman, 1981.

54 The tensions can be traced back to the beginning of the women's rights movement and the 1848 *Declaration of Sentiments*. Historians continue to analyze distinctions of race, class, and gender and the ways in which this triad of constructs complicated the abolitionist movement. Starting with the Seneca Falls Women's Rights Convention, commonalities in the class position and race of the abolitionists and reformers obscured differences between the activists and those they sought to protect, namely slaves – freed and bound – and poor women. The convention, spearheaded by five upper-middle-class white women reformers: Elizabeth Cady Stanton and Lucretia Mott, Martha Wright (Mott's sister), Jane Hunt and Mary Ann McCintock, produced the *Declaration of Sentiments*. This document shaped the women's rights movement. For a detailed discussion see Judith Wellman, "The Seneca Falls Women's Rights Convention: a Study of Social Networks," in Linda K. Kerber and Jane Sherron De Hart (eds.), *Women's America: Refocusing the Past*, 4th edn., New York: Oxford University Press, 1995, pp. 203–15. See also Rosenberg, *Divided Lives*, pp. 55–61.

55 See Ellen Carol DuBois, *Woman Suffrage and Women's Rights*. New York: New York University Press, 1998, and Suzanne Lebsock, "Woman Suffrage and White Supremacy: a Virginia Case Study," in Kerber and De Hart (eds.), *Women's America*, pp. 320–44.

56 See Paula Giddings, *When and Where I Enter: The Impact of Black Women on Race and Sex in America*, New York: Wm. Morrow, 1984, ch. 7.

57 Rosenberg, *Divided Lives*, p. 60.

58 Friedan, *The Feminine Mystique*; Eisenstein (ed.), *Capitalist Patriarchy and the Case for Socialist Feminism*.

59 Lerner, *Black Women in White America*; Giddings, *When and Where I Enter*; Darlene Clark Hine, *Black Women's History: Theory and Practice*, Black Women in United States History 9–10, Brooklyn, NY: Carlson, 1990.

60 See Hartsock, *Money, Sex, and Power*. In recent years standpoint theory has become the subject of lively debate: see Carolyn Allen and Judith A. Howard, *Provoking Feminisms*, Chicago: University of Chicago Press, 2000.

61 See Alexandre Kojève and Raymond Queneau, *Introduction to the Reading of Hegel*, New York: Basic Books, 1969; Karl Marx and Friedrich Engels, *The Marx–Engels Reader*, ed. Robert C. Tucker, New York: W. W. Norton, 1972; Michael Burawoy and Theda Skocpol (eds.), *Marxist Inquiries: Studies of Labor, Class, and States*, Chicago: University of Chicago Press, 1982; Jacques Derrida, *Specters of Marx: The State of the Debt, the Work of Mourning, and the New International*, New York: Routledge, 1994; and Saree Makdisi, Cesare Casarino, and Rebecca E. Karl, *Marxism beyond Marxism*, New York: Routledge, 1996.

62 Hartsock, *Money, Sex, and Power*.

63 Collins, *Black Feminist Thought*.

64 Judith Rollins, *Between Women: Domestics and Their Employers*, Labor and Social Change, Philadelphia: Temple University Press, 1985.

65 Erving Goffman, *Interaction Ritual: Essays in Face-to-Face Behavior*, Chicago: Aldine, 1967. See also Erving Goffman, *Encounters: Two Studies in the Sociology of Interaction*, Indianapolis: Bobbs-Merrill, 1961, and *Erving Goffman: Exploring the Interaction Order*, ed. Paul Drew and Anthony Wootton, Boston: Northeastern University Press, 1988.

66 See Arlie Russell Hochschild, "Love and Gold," in Barbara Ehrenreich and Arlie Russell Hochschild (eds.), *Global Woman: Nannies, Maids and Sex Workers in the New Economy*, New York: Owl Books, 2004, pp. 15–31.

67 See Pierrette Hondagneu-Sotelo, *Domestica: Immigrant Workers Cleaning and Caring in the Shadows of Influence*, Berkeley: University of California Press, 2001.

3 Complicating Race

1 See Clara E. Rodriguez, *Changing Race: Latinos, the Census, and the History of Ethnicity in the United States*, New York: New York University Press, 2000;

Robert Miles, *Racism*, Key Ideas, London and New York: Routledge, 1989; Paul Gilroy, *"There Ain't No Black the in Union Jack": The Cultural Politics of Race and Nation*, Black Literature and Culture, Chicago: University of Chicago Press, 1991; Paul Gilroy, *Against Race: Imagining Political Culture Beyond the Color Line*, Cambridge, Mass.: Belknap Press of Harvard University Press, 2000; Pierre L. Van den Berghe, *Race and Racism: A Comparative Perspective*, New York: John Wiley, 1967.

2   Judith Butler, *Gender Trouble: Feminism and the Subversion of Identity*, Thinking Gender, New York: Routledge, 1999.

3   Cornel West, *Race Matters*, Boston: Beacon Press, 1993.

4   Howard Winant, *Racial Conditions: Politics, Theory, Comparisons*, Minneapolis: University of Minnesota Press, 1994, p. 18.

5   See Stephen Jay Gould, *The Mismeasure of Man*, rev. and expanded edn., New York: W. W. Norton, 1996.

6   For a detailed discussion see Anthony W. Marx, *Making Race and Nation: A Comparison of South Africa, the United States, and Brazil*, Cambridge Studies in Comparative Politics, Cambridge and New York: Cambridge University Press, 1998.

7   Simone de Beauvoir, *The Second Sex*, New York: Vintage Books, 1974.

8   Michael Omi and Howard Winant, *Racial Formation in the United States: From the 1960s to the 1990s*, 2nd edn., New York: Routledge, 1994.

9   See Stephen Steinberg, *The Ethnic Myth: Race, Ethnicity, and Class in America*, updated and expanded edn., Boston: Beacon Press, 1989.

10   Eric Homberger, *The Historical Atlas of New York City*, New York: Henry Holt, 1994, p. 160; New York City Department of City Planning (2000), *The Newest New Yorkers: A Statistical Portrait*, New York, 2000; US Bureau of the Census, *2000 United States Decennial Census*, Washington, DC: US Government Printing Office, 2001.

11   Mary C. Waters, *Black Identities: West Indian Immigrant Dreams and American Realities*, 2nd edn., Cambridge, Mass.: Harvard University Press, 2001, p. 50.

12   Marx, *Making Race and Nation*, p. 252.

13   See Rodriguez, *Changing Race*.

14   Richard Graham (ed.), *The Idea of Race in Latin America, 1870–1940*, Austin: University of Texas Press, 1997. See also Winthrop R. Wright, *Café con Leche: Race Class, and National Image in Venezuela*, Austin: University of Texas Press, 1996.

15   Frank Dikotter (ed.), *The Construction of Racial Identity in China and Japan*, Hong Kong: Hong Kong University Press, 1997.

16   For a discussion of Southeast Asian, Asian Pacific, mainland Chinese and Japanese Americans, and other immigrant groups see Alejandro Portes and Rubén G. Rumbaut, *Immigrant America: A Portrait*, 2nd edn., Berkeley, Calif.: University of California Press, 1996.

17   Both view race as part of ethnicity and presume that ethnic groups are part of race groups, failing to differentiate between ethnic and racial inequality. See

Gunnar Myrdal's *An American Dilemma*, which focuses on questions of migration and cultural contact, and the ways in which ethnic groups come to interact with new societies: Gunnar Myrdal with Richard Mauritz Edvard Sterner and Arnold Marshall Rose, *An American Dilemma: The Negro Problem and Modern Democracy*, New York and London: Harper, 1944. See also Glazer and Moynihan for a discussion of cultural pluralism and political pluralism: Nathan Glazer and Daniel P. Moynihan, *Beyond the Melting Pot: The Negroes, Puerto Ricans, Jews, Italians, and Irish of New York City*, Cambridge, Mass.: MIT Press, 1963; Nathan Glazer and Daniel P. Moynihan, with Corinne Saposs Schelling (eds.), *Ethnicity: Theory and Experience*, Cambridge, Mass.: Harvard University Press, 1975; Daniel Patrick Moynihan, "The Negro Family: the Case for National Action," in Lee Rainwater and William C. Yancey, *The Moynihan Report and the Politics of Controversy*, Cambridge: MIT Press, 1967, chs. 2 and 4; Robert Ezra Park and Ernest Watson Burgess, *Introduction to the Science of Sociology, Including the Original Index to Basic Sociological Concepts*, 3rd edn., Chicago: University of Chicago Press, 1969; Horace Meyer Kallen, *Culture and Democracy in the United States*, New York: Boni & Liveright, 1924.

18 Stephan Thernstrom and American Council of Learned Societies, *The Other Bostonians: Poverty and Progress in the American Metropolis, 1880–1970*, Cambridge, Mass.: Harvard University Press, 1973, table 8.6, pp. 188, 190–4, 212, 257.

19 For a discussion of slavery see Peter Kolchin, *American Slavery, 1619–1877*, New York: Hill & Wang, 1994; Edmund Sears Morgan, *American Slavery, American Freedom: The Ordeal of Colonial Virginia*, New York: W. W. Norton, 1975; Leon F. Litwack, *North of Slavery: The Negro in the Free States, 1790–1860*, Chicago: University of Chicago Press, 1961; and Jacqueline Jones, *Labor of Love, Labor of Sorrow: Black Women, Work, and the Family from Slavery to the Present*, New York: Vintage Books, 1986.

20 George M. Fredrickson, *The Arrogance of Race: Historical Perspectives on Slavery, Racism, and Social Inequality*, Middletown, Conn.: Wesleyan University Press, 1988; Thomas F. Gossett, *Race: The History of an Idea in America*, New York: Schocken Books, 1965.

21 See Barbara Fields for a discussion on the use of "black" as a descriptor, "Ideology and Race in American History," in J. Morgan Kousser and James M. McPherson (eds.), *Region, Race, and Reconstruction: Essays in Honor of C. Vann Woodward*, New York: Oxford University Press, 1982. It should be noted that the tendency to collapse different ethnic groups under "black" obscures within-group differences. The lively debate on the subject can be found in the work of Thomas Sowell and Winston James in their analyses of differences among American-born and West Indian-born blacks over time (see Winston James, "Explaining Afro-Caribbean Social Mobility in the United States: Beyond the Sowell Thesis," *Comparative Studies in Society and History*, 44: 2 (Apr. 2002)).

22 Omi and Winant, *Racial Formation in the United States*, p. 24.

23 Ibid., p. 25.

24 Richard T. Selden (ed.), *Capitalism and Freedom: Problems and Prospects: Proceedings of a Conference in Honor of Milton Friedman*, Charlottesville: University Press of Virginia, 1975.

25 See Samuel Gompers, *American Federationist* (Sept. 1905), pp. 634–6, and Samuel Gompers, *The Samuel Gompers Papers*, ed. Stuart Bruce Kaufman, Urbana: University of Illinois Press, 1986.

26 Herbert George Gutman, *Work, Culture, and Society in Industrializing America: Essays in American Working-Class and Social History*, New York: Alfred A. Knopf, distr. Random House, 1975. For more recent analysis see Portes and Rumbaut, *Immigrant America*.

27 Omi and Winant, *Racial Formation in the United States*, p. 32.

28 See David R. Roediger, *The Wages of Whiteness: Race and the Making of the American Working Class*, London and New York: Verso, 1993; Stephen Steinberg, *Race and Ethnicity in the United States: Issues and Debates*, Oxford: Blackwell, 2000.

29 See Mary Pattillo-McCoy, *Black Picket Fences: Privilege and Peril among the Black Middle Class*, Chicago: University of Chicago Press, 1999.

30 William J. Wilson, *The Declining Significance of Race: Blacks and Changing American Institutions*, 2nd edn., Chicago: University of Chicago Press, 1980; William J. Wilson, *The Truly Disadvantaged: The Inner City, the Underclass, and Public Policy*, Chicago: University of Chicago Press, 1987; William J. Wilson, *When Work Disappears: The World of the New Urban Poor*, New York: Alfred A. Knopf, distr. Random House, 1996.

31 Omi and Winant, *Racial Formation in the United States*, p. 39.

32 Ibid., p. 38.

33 Ibid., pp. 38–9.

34 Harold Cruse, *The Crisis of the Negro Intellectual*, London: W. H. Allen, 1969.

35 Omi and Winant, *Racial Formation in the United States*, p. 43.

36 Stokely Carmichael and Charles V. Hamilton, *Black Power: The Politics of Liberation in America*, New York: Vintage Books, 1992; Bob Blauner, *Racial Oppression in America*, New York: Harper & Row, 1972.

37 Omi and Winant, *Racial Formation in the United States*, p. 45.

38 Paul A. Jargowsky, *Poverty and Place: Ghettos, Barrios, and the American City*, New York: Russell Sage Foundation, 1997.

39 Loïc J. D. Wacquant, "Race, Class and Space in Chicago and Paris," in Katherine McFate, Roger Lawson, and William J. Wilson (eds.), *Poverty, Inequality, and the Future of Social Policy: Western States in the New World Order*, New York: Russell Sage Foundation, 1995.

40 Loïc J. D. Waquant, "From Slavery to Mass Incarceration: Rethinking the 'Race Question' in the US," *New Left Review*, 13 (Jan.–Feb. 2002), 41–60. For further discussion see: "Ghetto," in Neil J. Smelser and Paul B. Baltes (eds.), *International Encyclopedia of the Social and Behavioral Sciences*, rev. edn., London: Pergamon Press, 2004, and "Decivilizing and Demonizing: Remaking the Black American

Ghetto," in Steven Loyal and Stephen Quilley (eds.), *The Sociology of Norbert Elias*, Cambridge: Cambridge University Press, 2004, pp. 95–121.

41 Ellis Cose, *The Rage of a Privileged Class*, New York: HarperPerennial, 1995.

42 See Roy L. Brooks, *Rethinking the American Race Problem*, Berkeley: University of California Press, 1990; Gilroy, *Against Race*; David Theo Goldberg, *Racist Culture: Philosophy and the Politics of Meaning*, Cambridge, Mass.: Blackwell, 1993; Miles, *Racism*.

43 Omi and Winant, *Racial Formation in the United States*, pp. 55–60; Winant, *Racial Conditions*.

44 Moynihan, "The Negro Family," chs. 2 and 4.

45 Oscar Lewis, *Five Families: Mexican Case Studies in the Culture of Poverty*, New York: Basic Books, 1959; Oscar Lewis, "The Culture of Poverty," *Scientific American*, 215 (Oct. 1966), p. 5.

46 Douglas S. Massey and Nancy A. Denton, *American Apartheid: Segregation and the Making of the Underclass*, Cambridge, Mass.: Harvard University Press, 1993.

47 See Pattillo-McCoy, *Black Picket Fences: Privilege and Peril among the Black Middle Class*.

48 See Herbert Hill and James E. Jones, *Race in America: The Struggle for Equality*, Madison: University of Wisconsin Press, 1993; Kimberle Crenshaw, Neil Gotanda, Gary Peller, and Kendall Thomas (eds.), *Critical Race Theory*, New York: New Press, 1995.

49 Ruth Sidel, *Keeping Women and Children Last: America's War on the Poor*, rev. edn., New York: Penguin Books, 1998, p. 143.

50 See Wacquant, "Race, Class and Space in Chicago and Paris."

51 Malcolm X, with Alex Haley, *The Autobiography of Malcolm X*, New York: Ballantine Books, 1999.

52 Matty Rich et al., *Straight Out of Brooklyn*, videorecording, HBO Video, New York, 1991.

53 Lynn S. Chancer, *Sadomasochism in Everyday Life: The Dynamics of Power and Powerlessness*, New Brunswick, NJ: Rutgers University Press, 1992.

54 R. W. Connell, *Masculinities*, Berkeley: University of California Press, 1995, p. 77.

55 Malcolm X, with Haley, *The Autobiography of Malcolm X*, pp. 17–22.

56 Michele Wallace, *Black Macho and the Myth of the Superwoman*, New York: Dial Press, 1979; Michele Wallace, *Black Macho and the Myth of Superwoman*, London and New York: Verso, 1990; Jargowsky, *Poverty and Place*.

57 Wallace, *Black Macho and the Myth of Superwoman*, p. 37.

58 Ibid., p. 110.

4 Class Matters

1 Stanley Aronowitz, *How Class Works: Power and Social Movement*, New Haven and London: Yale University Press, 2003, pp. 30–1, see also ch. 1 on "Class Matters."

2 Janny Scott and David Leonhardt, "Class in America: Shadowy Lines that Still Divide," *New York Times* (Sunday, May 15, 2005), front page.

3 Ibid., A26.

4 Ibid.

5 Ibid., p. 29.

6 Janny Scott, "Life at the Top in America isn't Just Better, It's Longer," *New York Times* (Monday, May 16, 2005), front page. The second article in the series, entitled "Life at the Top in America isn't Just Better, It's Longer," examines the issue of health disparities between the social classes, in particular cardiovascular disease.

7 Cornel West, *Race Matters*, Boston: Beacon Press, 1993.

8 Karl Marx and Friedrich Engels, *The German Ideology: Including Theses on Feuerbach and Introduction to the Critique of Political Economy*, Amherst, NY: Prometheus Books, 1998; Karl Marx and Friedrich Engels, *The Marx–Engels Reader*, ed. Robert C. Tucker, 2nd edn., New York: W. W. Norton, 1972.

9 Karl Marx, *Capital: A Critique of Political Economy*, trans. Ben Fowkes and David Fernbach. New York: Penguin Books with New Left Review, 1990.

10 Marx and Engels, *The Marx–Engels Reader*, p. 474.

11 Ibid., pp. 266–9.

12 Marshall Berman, *All That is Solid Melts into Air: The Experience of Modernity*, New York: Viking Penguin, 1988.

13 Marx, *Capital*; Marx and Engels, *The Marx–Engels Reader*.

14 Alexis de Tocqueville, *American Institutions and Their Influence*, with notes by John C. Spencer, New York: A. S. Barnes, 1855. Also see Alexis de Tocqueville, *Democracy in America, and Two Essays on America*, trans. Gerald E. Bevan, intro. Isaac Kramnick, London: Penguin, 2003.

15 Robert King Merton, *Social Theory and Social Structure*, enlarged edn., New York: Free Press, 1968; Lewis A. Coser (ed.), *The Idea of Social Structure: Papers in Honor of Robert K. Merton*, New York: Harcourt Brace Jovanovich, 1975.

16 Charles E. Reasons and Jack L. Kuykendall, *Race, Crime, and Justice*, Pacific Palisades, Calif.: Goodyear, 1972.

17 Edward S. Herman and Noam Chomsky, *Manufacturing Consent: The Political Economy of the Mass Media*, New York: Pantheon Books, 1988; Edward S. Herman, *The Myth of the Liberal Media: An Edward Herman Reader*, New York: P. Lang, 1999; Edward S. Herman and Robert Waterman McChesney, *The Global Media: The New Missionaries of Corporate Capitalism*, London and New York: Continuum, 2001; Noam Chomsky, *Necessary Illusions: Thought Control in Democratic Societies*, Boston: South End Press, 1989; Noam Chomsky et al., *Manufacturing Consent: Noam Chomsky and the Media*, videorecording, Zeitgeist Films, New York, 1994; Noam Chomsky, *Media Control: The Spectacular Achievements of Propaganda*, 2nd edn., New York: Seven Stories Press, 2002.

18 Steven R. Belenko, *Drugs and Drug Policy in America: A Documentary History*, Primary Documents in American History and Contemporary Issues, Westport, Conn.: Greenwood Press, 2000.

19 Richard Sennett and Jonathan Cobb, *The Hidden Injuries of Class*, New York: W. W. Norton, 1993; Michael Burawoy, *The Politics of Production: Factory Regimes under Capitalism and Socialism*, London: Verso, 1985; Harold L. Sheppard and Neal Q. Herrick, *Where Have All the Robots Gone? Worker Dissatisfaction in the '70s*, New York: Free Press, 1972.

20 Karl Marx and Friedrich Engels, *The Communist Manifesto, with Related Documents*, ed. John Edward Toews, Boston: Bedford, 1999.

21 For a discussion of dominant class tendencies to use superstructural social organizations to reproduce the division of labor see: Antonio Gramsci, *Selections from the Prison Notebooks of Antonio Gramsci*, ed. and trans. Quintin Hoare and Geoffrey Nowell-Smith, New York: International Publishers, 1971; Michel Foucault, *Discipline and Punish: The Birth of the Prison*, New York: Pantheon Books, 1977; Samuel Bowles and Herbert Gintis, *Schooling in Capitalist America: Educational Reform and the Contradictions of Economic Life*, New York: Basic Books, 1977.

22 Max Weber, *The Protestant Ethic and the Spirit of Capitalism*, Los Angeles: Roxbury, 2000, pp. 48–9.

23 Max Weber, *Economy and Society: An Outline of Interpretive Sociology*, ed. Guenther Roth and Claus Wittich, Berkeley: University of California Press, 1978.

24 Ibid.

25 Max Weber, *From Max Weber: Essays in Sociology*, trans. and ed. Hans Heinrich Gerth and C. Wright Mills, New York: Oxford University Press, 1969, pt. 3.

26 Weber, *The Protestant Ethic and the Spirit of Capitalism*.

27 Pierre Bourdieu and Loïc J. D. Wacquant, *An Invitation to Reflexive Sociology*, Chicago: University of Chicago Press, 1992.

28 Weber, *Economy and Society*, ch. 2.

29 Pierre Bourdieu, *Distinction: A Social Critique of the Judgement of Taste*, Cambridge, Mass.: Harvard University Press, 1984, p. 170.

30 Ibid., p. 172.

31 See Harrison C. White, *Markets from Networks: Socioeconomic Models of Production*, Princeton: Princeton University Press, 2002; Nan Lin, Karen S. Cook, and Ronald S. Burt, *Social Capital: Theory and Research*, Sociology and Economics, New York: Aldine de Gruyter, 2001; Lisa F. Berkman and Ichiro Kawachi, *Social Epidemiology*, New York: Oxford University Press, 2000; Gabriel Badescu and Eric M. Uslaner, *Social Capital and the Transition to Democracy*, Routledge Studies of Societies in Transition 20, London and New York: Routledge, 2003; Francisco Herreros, *The Problem of Forming Social Capital: Why Trust?* Political Evolution and Institutional Change, New York: Palgrave Macmillan, 2004; Bob Edwards, Michael W. Foley, and Mario Diani, *Beyond Tocqueville: Civil Society and the Social Capital Debate in Comparative Perspective*, Civil Society, Hanover, NH: University Press of New England for Tufts University, 2001.

32 Bourdieu notes: "scholastic success mainly depends on inherited cultural capital and on the propensity to invest in the educational system." He views educational institutions as hierarchical organizations reflecting the influence of the class. See Bourdieu, *Distinction*, p. 122.

33 Philippe I. Bourgois, *In Search of Respect: Selling Crack in El Barrio*, Structural Analysis in the Social Sciences, Cambridge and New York: Cambridge University Press, 1996.

34 Michael Omi and Howard Winant, *Racial Formation in the United States: From the 1960s to the 1990s*, 2nd edn., New York: Routledge, 1994.

35 Ibid., p. 13.

36 David R. Roediger, *The Wages of Whiteness: Race and the Making of the American Working Class*, London and New York: Verso, 1993.

37 See Paul Gilroy, *"There Ain't No Black in the Union Jack": The Cultural Politics of Race and Nation*, Black Literature and Culture, Chicago: University of Chicago Press, 1991; Samuel Gompers, *The Samuel Gompers Papers*, ed. Stuart Bruce Kaufman, Urbana: University of Illinois Press, 1986; Philip Sheldon Foner, *Organized Labor and the Black Worker, 1619–1981*, 2nd edn., New York: International Publishers, 1982; Philip Sheldon Foner and Ronald L. Lewis, *Black Workers: A Documentary History from Colonial Times to the Present*, Philadelphia: Temple University Press, 1989.

38 See the series of articles Herbert Hill wrote in *New Politics*: "Race, Ethnicity and Organized Labor: the Opposition to Affirmative Action," *New Politics*, 1: 2 (Winter 1987), pp. 31–82; "Meaney, Ruther and the 1964 Civil Rights Act," *New Politics*, 7: 1 (Summer 1998), pp. 83–107; "Lichtenstein's Fictions revisited: Race and the New Labor History," *New Politics*, 7: 2 (Winter 1999), pp. 149–63, and his "Race and the Steelworkers Union: White Privilege and Black Struggles," *New Politics*, 8: 4 (Winter 2002), pp. 175–207.

39 Barbara Ehrenreich, *Nickel and Dimed: On (Not) Getting By in America*, New York: Metropolitan Books, 2001.

40 Kathryn Edin and Laura Lein, *Making Ends Meet: How Single Mothers Survive Welfare and Low-Wage Work*, New York: Russell Sage Foundation, 1997, ch. 6.

41 See Leslie Salzinger, *Genders in Production: Making Workers in Mexico's Global Factories*, Berkeley: University of California Press, 2003.

5 Concluding Thoughts

1 Stanley Aronowitz, *How Class Works: Power and Social Movement*, New Haven and London: Yale University Press, 2003.

2 Robert R. Alford, *The Craft of Inquiry: Theories, Methods, Evidence*, New York: Oxford University Press, 1998.

3 Barbara Ehrenreich, *Nickel and Dimed: On (Not) Getting By in America*, New York: Metropolitan Books, 2001.

4   Lynn S. Chancer, *Reconcilable Differences: Confronting Beauty, Pornography, and the Future of Feminism*, Berkeley: University of California Press, 1998.

5   Stanley Aronowitz and William DiFazio, *The Jobless Future: Sci-Tech and the Dogma of Work*, Minneapolis: University of Minnesota Press, 1994.

6   Douglas S. Massey and Nancy A. Denton, *American Apartheid: Segregation and the Making of the Underclass*, Cambridge, Mass.: Harvard University Press, 1993.

7   Lynn S. Chancer, *Sadomasochism in Everyday Life: The Dynamics of Power and Powerlessness*, New Brunswick, NJ: Rutgers University Press, 1992.

8   Erich Fromm, *Escape from Freedom*, New York: Henry Holt, 1994.

9   Philippe I. Bourgois, *In Search of Respect: Selling Crack in El Barrio*, Cambridge and New York: Cambridge University Press, 1996.

10 R. W. Connell, *Masculinities*, Berkeley: University of California Press, 1995.

11 Lynn S. Chancer, *High-Profile Crimes: When Legal Cases Become Social Causes*, Chicago: University of Chicago Press, 2005.

Bibliography

I Why Gender, Race, and Class?

Andersen, Margaret L., and Patricia Hill Collins (comps.). *Race, Class, and Gender: An Anthology*. 3rd edn. Belmont, Calif.: Wadsworth, 1998.

Berger, John. *Ways of Seeing*. London and New York: BBC/Penguin Books, 1991.

Berger, Peter L., and Thomas Luckmann. *The Social Construction of Reality: A Treatise in the Sociology of Knowledge*. Garden City, NY: Doubleday, 1966.

Bourgois, Philippe I. *In Search of Respect: Selling Crack in El Barrio*. Cambridge and New York: Cambridge University Press, 1996.

Butler, Judith. *Gender Trouble: Feminism and the Subversion of Identity*. New York: Routledge, 1990.

Chancer, Lynn S. *Sadomasochism in Everyday Life: The Dynamics of Power and Powerlessness*. New Brunswick, NJ: Rutgers University Press, 1992.

Cohen, Stanley. *Folk Devils and Moral Panics: The Creation of the Mods and Rockers*. Oxford: Blackwell, 1987.

Durkheim, Emile. *The Rules of Sociological Method, and Selected Texts on Sociology and Its Method*, ed. Steven Lukes. London: Macmillan, 1982.

Faludi, Susan. *Backlash: The Undeclared War against American Women*. New York: Crown, 1991.

Firestone, Shulamith. *The Dialectic of Sex: The Case for Feminist Revolution*. London: Women's Press, 1979.

Fischer, Claude S., et al. *Inequality by Design: Cracking the Bell Curve Myth*. Princeton: Princeton University Press, 1996.

Freud, Sigmund. *Civilization and Its Discontents*. New York: W. W. Norton, 1989.

Goffman, Erving. *The Goffman Reader*, ed. Charles C. Lemert and Ann Branaman. Cambridge, Mass.: Blackwell, 1997.

Herrnstein, Richard J., and Charles Murray, *The Bell Curve: Intelligence and Class Structure in American Life*. New York: Free Press, 1994.

Jankowski, Martín Sánchez. *City Bound: Urban Life and Political Attitudes among Chicano Youth*. Albuquerque: University of New Mexico Press, 1986.

——. *Islands in the Street: Gangs and American Urban Society*. Berkeley: University of California Press, 1991.

Katz, Jack. *How Emotions Work*. Chicago: University of Chicago Press, 1999.

—— . *Seductions of Crime: Moral and Sensual Attractions in Doing Evil*. New York: Basic Books, 1988.

Lorenz, Konrad. *On Aggression*. New York: Harcourt, Brace & World, 1996.

Millett, Kate. *Sexual Politics*. Garden City, NY: Doubleday, 1970.

Mills, C. Wright. *The Sociological Imagination*. New York: Oxford University Press, 2000.

Steinberg, Stephen. *Turning Back: The Retreat from Racial Justice in American Policy and Thought*. Boston: Beacon Press, 1996.

Wilson, William Julius. *The Declining Significance of Race: Blacks and Changing American Institutions*, 2nd edn. Chicago: University of Chicago Press, 1980.

—— . *The Truly Disadvantaged: The Inner City, the Underclass, and Public Policy*. Chicago: University of Chicago Press, 1987.

—— . *When Work Disappears: The World of the New Urban Poor*. New York: Alfred A. Knopf, distr. by Random House, 1996.

2 Gender Defined and Refined

Allen, Carolyn, and Judith A. Howard. *Provoking Feminisms*. Chicago: University of Chicago Press, 2000.

Antrobus, Peggy. *The Global Women's Movement: Origins, Issues and Strategies*. London: Zed Books, 2004.

Anzaldúa, Gloria. *Making Face, Making Soul/Haciendo Caras: Creative and Critical Perspectives by Women of Color*, 1st edn. San Francisco: Aunt Lute Foundation Books, 1990.

Aristophanes. *Lysistrata*, trans. Douglass Parker. New York: Signet Classic, 2001.

Atkinson, Ti-Grace. *Amazon Odyssey: Collection of Writings*. New York: Links Books; distr. Quick Fox, 1974.

Barrett, Michèle. *Women's Oppression Today: Problems in Marxist Feminist Analysis*. London: New Left Books, 1980.

Barrios de Chungara, Domitila, and Moema Viezzer. *Let Me Speak! Testimony of Domitila, a Woman of the Bolivian Mines*. New York: Monthly Review Press, 1978.

Beauvoir, Simone de. *The Second Sex*. New York: Vintage Books, 1974.

Benjamin, Jessica. *The Bonds of Love: Psychoanalysis, Feminism, and the Problem of Domination*. New York: Pantheon Books, 1988.

Berry, Mary Frances. *Why ERA Failed: Politics, Women's Rights, and the Amending Process of the Constitution*. Everywoman. Bloomington: Indiana University Press, 1986.

Boston Women's Health Book Collective. *Our Bodies, Ourselves*. New York: Simon & Schuster, 1973.

Brownmiller, Susan. *Against Our Will: Men, Women, and Rape*. New York: Simon & Schuster, 1975.

Burawoy, Michael, and Theda Skocpol (eds.). *Marxist Inquiries: Studies of Labor, Class, and States*. Chicago: University of Chicago Press, 1982.

Butler, Judith. *Gender Trouble: Feminism and the Subversion of Identity*. Thinking Gender. New York: Routledge, 1990.

Chancer, Lynn S. *Sadomasochism in Everyday Life: The Dynamics of Power and Powerlessness*. New Brunswick, NJ: Rutgers University Press, 1992.

—— . *Reconcilable Differences: Confronting Beauty, Pornography, and the Future of Feminism*. Berkeley: University of California Press, 1998.

Chavez-Garcia, Miroslava. *Negotiating Conquest: Gender and Power in California, 1770s to 1880s*. Tucson: University of Arizona Press, 2004.

Chodorow, Nancy. *The Reproduction of Mothering: Psychoanalysis and the Sociology of Gender*. Berkeley: University of California Press, 1978.

Collins, Patricia Hill. *Black Feminist Thought: Knowledge, Consciousness, and the Politics of Empowerment*. Perspectives on Gender 2. Boston: Unwin Hyman, 1990.

—— . *Black Sexual Politics: African Americans, Gender, and the New Racism*. New York: Routledge, 2004.

Cott, Nancy. "Historical Perspectives: the Equal Rights Amendment in the 1920s." In Marianne Hirsch and Evelyn Fox Keller (eds.), *Conflicts in Feminism*. New York: Routledge, 1990.

Cowan, Ruth Schwartz. *More Work for Mother: The Ironies of Household Technology from the Open Hearth to the Microwave*. New York: Basic Books, 1983.

Derrida, Jacques. *Specters of Marx: The State of the Debt, the Work of Mourning, and the New International*. New York: Routledge, 1994.

DuBois, Ellen Carol. *Woman Suffrage and Women's Rights*. New York: New York University Press, 1998.

Durkheim, Emile, et al. *The Rules of Sociological Method*, 8th edn. Glencoe, Ill.: Free Press, 1950.

Echols, Alice. *Daring to Be Bad: Radical Feminism in America, 1967–1975*. Minneapolis: University of Minnesota Press, 1989.

Eisenstein, Zillah R. *The Radical Future of Liberal Feminism*. Longman Series in Feminist Theory. New York: Longman, 1981.

—— (ed.). *Capitalist Patriarchy and the Case for Socialist Feminism*. New York: Monthly Review Press, 1978.

Engels, Friedrich. *The Origin of the Family, Private Property, and the State, in the Light of the Researches of Lewis H. Morgan*, intro. and notes by Eleanor Burke Leacock, 1st edn. New York: International Publishers, 1972.

Evans, Sara M. *Personal Politics: The Roots of Women's Liberation in the Civil Rights Movement and the New Left*. New York: Vintage Books, 1980.

Fineman, Martha, and Nancy Sweet Thomadsen. *At the Boundaries of Law: Feminism and Legal Theory*. New York: Routledge, 1991.

Firestone, Shulamith. *The Dialectic of Sex: The Case for Feminist Revolution*. London: Women's Press, 1979.

Freeman, Jo. *The Politics of Women's Liberation: A Case Study of an Emerging Social Movement and Its Relation to the Policy Process*. New York: McKay, 1975.

Friedan, Betty. *The Feminine Mystique*. New York: W. W. Norton, 1983.

——— . *It Changed My Life: Writings on the Women's Movement*. Cambridge, Mass.: Harvard University Press, 1998.

Fuchs, Victor R. *Women's Quest for Economic Equality*. Cambridge, Mass.: Harvard University Press, 1988.

Giddings, Paula. *When and Where I Enter: The Impact of Black Women on Race and Sex in America*. New York: Wm. Morrow, 1984.

Glenn, Evelyn Nakano. *Issei, Nisei, War Bride: Three Generations of Japanese American Women in Domestic Service*. Philadelphia: Temple University Press, 1986.

——— . *Unequal Freedom: How Race and Gender Shaped American Citizenship and Labor*. Cambridge, Mass. and London: Harvard University Press, 2002.

Goffman, Erving. *Encounters: Two Studies in the Sociology of Interaction*. Indianapolis: Bobbs-Merrill, 1961.

——— . *Interaction Ritual: Essays in Face-to-Face Behavior*. Chicago: Aldine, 1967.

——— . *Erving Goffman: Exploring the Interaction Order*, ed. Paul Drew and Anthony Wootton. Boston: Northeastern University Press, 1988.

Goldin, Claudia Dale. *Understanding the Gender Gap: An Economic History of American Women*. New York: Oxford University Press, 1990.

Gordon, Linda. *Pitied but Not Entitled: Single Mothers and the History of Welfare, 1890–1935*. New York: Free Press; Toronto: Maxwell Macmillan Canada, 1994.

Harding, Sandra G. *The Science Question in Feminism*. Ithaca, NY: Cornell University Press, 1986.

Hartsock, Nancy C. M. *Money, Sex, and Power: Toward a Feminist Historical Materialism*. Northeastern Series in Feminist Theory. Boston: Northeastern University Press, 1985.

Hennessy, Rosemary, and Chrys Ingraham. *Materialist Feminism: A Reader in Class, Difference, and Women's Lives*. New York: Routledge, 1997.

Hine, Darlene Clark. *Black Women's History: Theory and Practice*. Black Women in United States History 9–10. Brooklyn, NY: Carlson, 1990.

Hochschild, Arlie Russell. *The Second Shift: Working Parents and the Revolution at Home*. New York, NY: Viking, 1989.

——— . "Love and Gold." In Barbara Ehrenreich and Arlie Russell Hochschild (eds.), *Global Woman: Nannies, Maids and Sex Workers in the New Economy*. New York: Owl Books, 2004

Hole, Judith, and Ellen Levine. *Rebirth of Feminism*. New York: Quadrangle Books, 1973.

Hondagneu-Sotelo, Pierrette. *Domestica: Immigrant Workers Cleaning and Caring in the Shadows of Influence*. Berkeley: University of California Press, 2001.

Hooks, Bell. *Ain't I a Woman: Black Women and Feminism*. Boston: South End Press, 1981.

——— . *Feminist Theory from Margin to Center*. Boston: South End Press, 1984.

Keller, Evelyn Fox, and Helen E. Longino. *Feminism and Science*. Oxford Readings in Feminism. Oxford and New York: Oxford University Press, 1996.

Kerber, Linda K., and Jane Sherron De Hart (eds.). *Women's America: Refocusing the Past*, 4th edn. New York: Oxford University Press, 1995.

Kessler, Suzanne J., and Wendy McKenna. *Gender: An Ethnomethodological Approach*. New York: John Wiley, 1978.

Kessler-Harris, Alice. *Out to Work: A History of Wage-Earning Women in the United States*. New York: Oxford University Press, 1982.

Kingston, Maxine Hong. *The Woman Warrior: Memoirs of a Girlhood among Ghosts*. New York: Vintage Books, 1989.

Kingston, Maxine Hong, Luisa Valenzuela, and Stephanie Dowrick. *Two Foreign Women: Maxine Hong Kingston, Luisa Valenzuela*. Leichhardt, NSW: Pluto Press, 1990.

Kojève, Alexandre, and Raymond Queneau. *Introduction to the Reading of Hegel*. New York: Basic Books, 1969.

Lemert, Edwin McCarthy. *Human Deviance, Social Problems, and Social Control*. Englewood Cliffs, NJ: Prentice-Hall, 1967.

Lerner, Gerda (ed.). *Black Women in White America: A Documentary History*. New York: Vintage Books, 1973.

Luker, Kristin. *Abortion and the Politics of Motherhood*. California Series on Social Choice and Political Economy. Berkeley: University of California Press, 1984.

Maher, Lisa. *Sexed Work: Gender, Race, and Resistance in a Brooklyn Drug Market*. Clarendon Studies in Criminology. Oxford and New York: Clarendon Press, 1997.

Mahler, Margaret S., Anni Bergman, and Mahler Research Foundation. *The Psychological Birth of the Human Infant: The Separation-Individuation Process*. video recording. Mahler Research Foundation, Franklin Lakes, NJ, 1983.

Makdisi, Saree, Cesare Casarino, and Rebecca E. Karl. *Marxism beyond Marxism*. New York: Routledge, 1996.

Mansbridge, Jane J. *Why We Lost the ERA*. Chicago: University of Chicago Press, 1986.

Marx, Karl, and Friedrich Engels. *The Marx–Engels Reader*, ed. Robert C. Tucker. New York: W. W. Norton, 1972.

Milkman, Ruth. *Gender at Work: The Dynamics of Job Segregation by Sex during World War II*. Urbana: University of Illinois Press, 1987.

—— . *Women, Work, and Protest: A Century of US Women's Labor History*. Boston: Routledge & Kegan Paul, 1985.

Mill, John Stuart. *The Subjection of Women*, ed. Susan Moller Okin. Indianapolis: Hackett, 1988.

Millett, Kate. *Sexual Politics*, 1st edn. Garden City, NY: Doubleday, 1970.

Mitchell, Juliet. *Woman's Estate*. New York: Pantheon Books, 1972.

Morgan, Lewis Henry, *Ancient Society, or, Researches in the Lines of Human Progress from Savagery through Barbarism to Civilization*, ed. by Eleanor Burke Leacock. Gloucester, Mass.: P. Smith, 1974.

Oakley, Ann. *Woman's Work: The Housewife, Past and Present*. New York: Pantheon Books, 1975.

Ortner, Sherry. "Is Female to Male as Nature is to Culture?" In Michelle Zimbalist Rosaldo and Louise Lamphere (eds.), *Women, Culture and Society*. Stanford, Calif.: Stanford University Press, 1974, pp. 67–87.

Pateman, Carole. *The Sexual Contract*. Stanford, Calif.: Stanford University Press, 1988.

Ratner, Mitchell S. *Crack Pipe as Pimp: An Ethnographic Investigation of Sex-for-Crack Exchanges*. New York: Lexington Books; Toronto: Maxwell Macmillan Canada, 1993.

Rollins, Judith. *Between Women: Domestics and Their Employers*. Labor and Social Change. Philadelphia: Temple University Press, 1985.

Rosenberg, Rosalind. *Divided Lives: American Women in the Twentieth Century*, Introduction by Eric Foner. American Century Series. New York: Hill & Wang, 1992.

Rowbotham, Sheila. *Woman's Consciousness, Man's World*. Harmondsworth: Penguin, 1973.

Russell, Diana E. H. *Rape in Marriage*. New York: Collier Books, 1983.

Spivak, Gayatri Chakravorty. *In Other Worlds: Essays in Cultural Politics*. New York: Methuen, 1987.

—— . *Thinking Academic Freedom in Gendered Post-Coloniality*. Cape Town: University of Cape Town, 1992.

Steinberg, Ronnie. *Wages and Hours: Labor and Reform in Twentieth-Century America*. New Brunswick, NJ: Rutgers University Press, 1982.

Steinberg, Ronnie, Deborah M. Figart, and American Academy of Political and Social Science. *Emotional Labor in the Service Economy*. Annals of the American Academy of Political and Social Science 561. Thousand Oaks, Calif.: Sage Publications, 1999.

Trinh, T. Minh-Ha. *When the Moon Waxes Red: Representation, Gender, and Cultural Politics*. New York: Routledge, 1991.

—— . *Woman, Native, Other: Writing Postcoloniality and Feminism*. Bloomington: Indiana University Press, 1989.

West, Candace, and Don H. Zimmerman. "Doing Gender." *Gender and Society*, 1: 2 (June 1987), pp.125–51.

Wollstonecraft, Mary. *A Vindication of the Rights of Women*. Buffalo, NY: Prometheus Books, 1989.

3   Complicating Race

Beauvoir, Simone de. *The Second Sex*. New York: Vintage Books, 1974.

Blauner, Bob. *Racial Oppression in America*. New York: Harper & Row, 1972.

Brooks, Roy L. *Rethinking the American Race Problem*. Berkeley: University of California Press, 1990.

Butler, Judith. *Gender Trouble: Feminism and the Subversion of Identity*. Thinking Gender. New York: Routledge, 1999.

Carmichael, Stokely, and Charles V. Hamilton. *Black Power: The Politics of Liberation in America*. New York: Vintage Books, 1992.

Chancer, Lynn S. *Sadomasochism in Everyday Life: The Dynamics of Power and Powerlessness*. New Brunswick, NJ: Rutgers University Press, 1992.

Connell, R. W. *Masculinities*. Berkeley: University of California Press, 1995.

Cose, Ellis. *The Rage of a Privileged Class*. New York: HarperPerennial, 1995.

Crenshaw, Kimberle, Neil Gotanda, Gary Peller, and Kendall Thomas (eds.). *Critical Race Theory*. New York: New Press, 1995.

Cruse, Harold. *The Crisis of the Negro Intellectual*. London: W. H. Allen, 1969.

Dikotter, Frank (ed.). *The Construction of Racial Identity in China and Japan*. Hong Kong: Hong Kong University Press, 1997.

Fields, Barbara, "Ideology and Race in American History." In J. Morgan Kousser and James M. McPherson (eds.), *Region, Race, and Reconstruction: Essays in Honor of C. Vann Woodward*. New York: Oxford University Press, 1982.

Fredrickson, George M. *The Arrogance of Race: Historical Perspectives on Slavery, Racism, and Social Inequality*. Middletown, Conn.: Wesleyan University Press, 1988.

Gilroy, Paul. *"There Ain't No Black in the Union Jack": The Cultural Politics of Race and Nation*. Black Literature and Culture. Chicago: University of Chicago Press, 1991.

—— . *Against Race: Imagining Political Culture beyond the Color Line*. Cambridge, Mass.: Belknap Press of Harvard University Press, 2000.

Glazer, Nathan, and Daniel P. Moynihan. *Beyond the Melting Pot: The Negroes, Puerto Ricans, Jews, Italians, and Irish of New York City*. Cambridge, Mass.: MIT Press, 1963.

Glazer, Nathan, Daniel P. Moynihan, with Corinne Saposs Schelling (eds.). *Ethnicity: Theory and Experience*. Cambridge, Mass.: Harvard University Press, 1975.

Goldberg, David Theo. *Racist Culture: Philosophy and the Politics of Meaning*. Oxford: Blackwell, 1993.

Gompers, Samuel. *The Samuel Gompers Papers*, ed. Stuart Bruce Kaufman. Urbana: University of Illinois Press, 1986.

Gossett, Thomas F. *Race: The History of an Idea in America*. New York: Schocken Books, 1965.

Gould, Stephen Jay. *The Mismeasure of Man*, rev. and expanded edn. New York: W. W. Norton, 1996.

Graham, Richard (ed.). *The Idea of Race in Latin America, 1870–1940*. Austin: University of Texas Press, 1997.

Gutman, Herbert George. *Work, Culture, and Society in Industrializing America: Essays in American Working-Class and Social History*. New York: Alfred A. Knopf, distr. Random House, 1975.

Hill, Herbert, and James E. Jones. *Race in America: The Struggle for Equality*. Madison: University of Wisconsin Press, 1993.

Homberger, Eric. *The Historical Atlas of New York City*. New York: Henry Holt, 1994.

James, Winston. "Explaining Afro-Caribbean Social Mobility in the United States: Beyond the Sowell Thesis," *Comparative Studies in Society and History*, 44: 2 (Apr. 2002).

Jargowsky, Paul A. *Poverty and Place: Ghettos, Barrios, and the American City*. New York: Russell Sage Foundation, 1997.

Jones, Jacqueline. *Labor of Love, Labor of Sorrow: Black Women, Work, and the Family from Slavery to the Present*. New York: Vintage Books, 1986.

Kallen, Horace Meyer. *Culture and Democracy in the United States*. New York: Boni & Liveright, 1924.

Kolchin, Peter. *American Slavery, 1619–1877*. New York: Hill & Wang, 1994.

Lewis, Oscar. *Five Families: Mexican Case Studies in the Culture of Poverty*. New York: Basic Books, 1959.

——— . "The Culture of Poverty." *Scientific American*, 215 (Oct. 1966).

Litwack, Leon F. *North of Slavery: The Negro in the Free States, 1790–1860*. Chicago: University of Chicago Press, 1961.

Loyal, Steven, and Stephen Quilley (eds.). *The Sociology of Norbert Elias*. Cambridge: Cambridge University Press, 2004.

McFate, Katherine, Roger Lawson, and William J. Wilson. *Poverty, Inequality, and the Future of Social Policy: Western States in the New World Order*. New York: Russell Sage Foundation, 1995.

Marx, Anthony W. *Making Race and Nation: A Comparison of South Africa, the United States, and Brazil*. Cambridge Studies in Comparative Politics. Cambridge and New York: Cambridge University Press, 1998.

Massey, Douglas S., and Nancy A. Denton. *American Apartheid: Segregation and the Making of the Underclass*. Cambridge, Mass.: Harvard University Press, 1993.

Miles, Robert. *Racism*. Key Ideas. London and New York: Routledge, 1989.

Morgan, Edmund Sears. *American Slavery, American Freedom: The Ordeal of Colonial Virginia*. New York: W. W. Norton, 1975.

Moynihan, Daniel Patrick. "The Negro Family: the Case for National Action." In Lee Rainwater and William C. Yancey (eds.), *The Moynihan Report and the Politics of Controversy*, Cambridge, Mass.: MIT Press, 1967.

Myrdal, Gunnar, with Richard Mauritz Edvard Sterner and Arnold Marshall Rose. *An American Dilemma: The Negro Problem and Modern Democracy*. New York and London: Harper, 1944.

New York City Department of City Planning. *The Newest New Yorkers: A Statistical Portrait*. New York, 2000.

Omi, Michael, and Howard Winant. *Racial Formation in the United States: From the 1960s to the 1990s*. 2nd edn. New York: Routledge, 1994.

Park, Robert Ezra, and Ernest Watson Burgess. *Introduction to the Science of Sociology, Including the Original Index to Basic Sociological Concepts*, 3rd edn. Chicago: University of Chicago Press, 1969.

Pattillo-McCoy, Mary. *Black Picket Fences: Privilege and Peril among the Black Middle Class*. Chicago: University of Chicago Press, 1999.

Portes, Alejandro, and Rubén G. Rumbaut. *Immigrant America: A Portrait*, 2nd edn. Berkeley, Calif.: University of California Press, 1996.

Rich, Matty, et al. *Straight Out of Brooklyn*. Videorecording. HBO Video, New York, 1991.

Rodriguez, Clara E. *Changing Race: Latinos, the Census, and the History of Ethnicity in the United States*. New York: New York University Press, 2000.

Roediger, David R. *The Wages of Whiteness: Race and the Making of the American Working Class*. London and New York: Verso, 1993.

Rollins, Judith. *Between Women: Domestics and Their Employers*. Labor and Social Change. Philadelphia: Temple University Press, 1985.

Selden, Richard T. (ed.), *Capitalism and Freedom: Problems and Prospects: Proceedings of a Conference in Honor of Milton Friedman*. Charlottesville: University Press of Virginia, 1975.

Sidel, Ruth. *Keeping Women and Children Last: America's War on the Poor*, rev. edn. New York: Penguin Books, 1998.

Steinberg, Stephen. *The Ethnic Myth: Race, Ethnicity, and Class in America*, updated and expanded edn. Boston: Beacon Press, 1989.

—— . *Race and Ethnicity in the United States: Issues and Debates*. Malden, Mass.: Blackwell, 2000.

Thernstrom, Stephan, and American Council of Learned Societies. *The Other Bostonians: Poverty and Progress in the American Metropolis, 1880–1970*. Cambridge, Mass.: Harvard University Press, 1973.

Toynbee, Arnold Joseph. *A Study of History*, new edn. New York: Oxford University Press, distr. American Heritage Press, 1972.

US Bureau of the Census. *2000 United States Decennial Census*. Washington, DC: US Government Printing Office, 2001.

Van den Berghe, Pierre L. *Race and Racism: A Comparative Perspective*. New York: Wiley, 1967.

Wacquant, Loïc J. D. "Race, Class and Space in Chicago and Paris." In Katherine McFate, Roger Lawson, and William J. Wilson (eds.), *Poverty, Inequality, and the Future of Social Policy: Western States in the New World Order*. New York: Russell Sage Foundation, 1995.

—— "From Slavery to Mass Incarceration: Rethinking the 'Race Question' in the US." *New Left Review*, 13 (Jan.–Feb. 2002), 41–60.

Wallace, Michele. *Black Macho and the Myth of the Superwoman*. New York: Dial Press, 1979.

—— . *Black Macho and the Myth of Superwoman*. London and New York: Verso, 1990.

Waters, Mary C. *Black Identities: West Indian Immigrant Dreams and American Realities*, 2nd edn. Cambridge, Mass.: Harvard University Press, 2001.

West, Cornel. *Race Matters*. Boston: Beacon Press, 1993.

Wilson, William J. *The Declining Significance of Race: Blacks and Changing American Institutions*, 2nd edn. Chicago: University of Chicago Press, 1980.

—— . *The Truly Disadvantaged: The Inner City, the Underclass, and Public Policy*. Chicago: University of Chicago Press, 1987.

—— . *When Work Disappears: The World of the New Urban Poor*. New York: Alfred A. Knopf, distr. Random House, 1996.

Winant, Howard. *Racial Conditions: Politics, Theory, Comparisons*. Minneapolis: University of Minnesota Press, 1994.

Wright, Winthrop R. *Café con Leche: Race Class, and National Image in Venezuela*. Austin: University of Texas Press, 1996.

X, Malcolm, with Alex Haley. *The Autobiography of Malcolm X*. New York: Ballantine Books, 1999.

4 Class Matters

Aronowitz, Stanley. *How Class Works: Power and Social Movement*. New Haven and London: Yale University Press, 2003.

Badescu, Gabriel, and Eric M. Uslaner. *Social Capital and the Transition to Democracy*. Routledge Studies of Societies in Transition 20. London: Routledge, 2003.

Belenko, Steven R. *Drugs and Drug Policy in America: A Documentary History*. Primary Documents in American History and Contemporary Issues. Westport, Conn.: Greenwood Press, 2000.

Berkman, Lisa F., and Ichiro Kawachi. *Social Epidemiology*. New York: Oxford University Press, 2000.

Berman, Marshall. *All That is Solid Melts into Air: The Experience of Modernity*. New York: Viking Penguin, 1988.

Bourdieu, Pierre. *Distinction: A Social Critique of the Judgement of Taste*. Cambridge, Mass.: Harvard University Press, 1984.

Bourdieu, Pierre, and Loïc J. D. Wacquant. *An Invitation to Reflexive Sociology*. Chicago: University of Chicago Press, 1992.

Bourgois, Philippe I. *In Search of Respect: Selling Crack in El Barrio*. Structural Analysis in the Social Sciences. Cambridge and New York: Cambridge University Press, 1996.

Bowles, Samuel, and Herbert Gintis. *Schooling in Capitalist America: Educational Reform and the Contradictions of Economic Life*. New York: Basic Books, 1977.

Burawoy, Michael. *The Politics of Production: Factory Regimes under Capitalism and Socialism*. London: Verso, 1985.

Chomsky, Noam. *Necessary Illusions: Thought Control in Democratic Societies*. Boston: South End Press, 1989.

——— . *Media Control: The Spectacular Achievements of Propaganda*, 2nd edn. New York: Seven Stories Press, 2002.

Chomsky, Noam, et al. *Manufacturing Consent: Noam Chomsky and the Media*. Videorecording. Zeitgeist Films, New York, 1994.

Coser, Lewis A. (ed.). *The Idea of Social Structure: Papers in Honor of Robert K. Merton*. New York: Harcourt Brace Jovanovich, 1975.

Edin, Kathryn, and Laura Lein. *Making Ends Meet: How Single Mothers Survive Welfare and Low-Wage Work*. New York: Russell Sage Foundation, 1997.

Edwards, Bob, Michael W. Foley, and Mario Diani. *Beyond Tocqueville: Civil Society and the Social Capital Debate in Comparative Perspective*. Civil Society. Hanover, NH: University Press of New England for Tufts University, 2001.

Ehrenreich, Barbara. *Nickel and Dimed: On (Not) Getting By in America*. New York: Metropolitan Books, 2001.

Foner, Philip Sheldon. *Organized Labor and the Black Worker, 1619–1981*, 2nd edn. New York: International Publishers, 1982.

Foner, Philip Sheldon, and Ronald L. Lewis (eds.). *Black Workers: A Documentary History from Colonial Times to the Present*. Philadelphia: Temple University Press, 1989.

Foucault, Michel. *Discipline and Punish: The Birth of the Prison*. New York: Pantheon Books, 1977.

Gilroy, Paul. *"There Ain't No Black in the Union Jack": The Cultural Politics of Race and Nation*. Black Literature and Culture. Chicago: University of Chicago Press, 1991.

Gompers, Samuel. *The Samuel Gompers Papers*, ed. Stuart Bruce Kaufman. Urbana: University of Illinois Press, 1986.

Gramsci, Antonio. *Selections from the Prison Notebooks of Antonio Gramsci*, ed. and trans. Quintin Hoare and Geoffrey Nowell-Smith. New York: International Publishers, 1971.

Herman, Edward S. *The Myth of the Liberal Media: An Edward Herman Reader*. New York: P. Lang, 1999.

Herman, Edward S., and Noam Chomsky. *Manufacturing Consent: The Political Economy of the Mass Media*. New York: Pantheon Books, 1988.

Herman, Edward S., and Robert Waterman McChesney. *The Global Media: The New Missionaries of Corporate Capitalism*. London and New York: Continuum, 2001.

Herreros, Francisco. *The Problem of Forming Social Capital: Why Trust?* Political Evolution and Institutional Change. New York: Palgrave Macmillan, 2004.

Hill, Herbert. "Race, Ethnicity and Organized Labor: the Opposition to Affirmative Action." *New Politics*, 1: 2 (Winter 1987), pp. 31–82.

——. "Meaney, Ruther and the 1964 Civil Rights Act." *New Politics*, 7: 1 (Summer 1998), pp. 83–107.

——. "Lichtenstein's Fictions Revisited: Race and the New Labor History." *New Politics*, 7: 2 (Winter 1999), pp. 149–63.

——. "Race and the Steelworkers Union: White Privilege and Black Struggles." *New Politics*, 8: 4 (Winter 2002), pp. 175–207.

Lin, Nan, Karen S. Cook, and Ronald S. Burt. *Social Capital: Theory and Research*. Sociology and Economics. New York: Aldine de Gruyter, 2001.

Marx, Karl. *Capital: A Critique of Political Economy*, trans. Ben Fowkes and David Fernbach. New York: Penguin Books with New Left Review, 1990.

Marx, Karl, and Friedrich Engels. *The German Ideology: Including Theses on Feuerbach and Introduction to the Critique of Political Economy*. Amherst, NY: Prometheus Books, 1998.

Marx, Karl, and Friedrich Engels. *The Marx–Engels Reader*, ed. Robert C. Tucker. 2nd edn. New York: W. W. Norton, 1972.

Marx, Karl, and Friedrich Engels. *The Communist Manifesto: With Related Documents*, ed. John Edward Toews. Boston: Bedford, 1999.

Merton, Robert King. *Social Theory and Social Structure*, enlarged edn. New York: Free Press, 1968.

Omi, Michael, and Howard Winant. *Racial Formation in the United States: From the 1960s to the 1990s*, 2nd edn. New York: Routledge, 1994.

Reasons, Charles E., and Jack L. Kuykendall. *Race, Crime, and Justice*. Pacific Palisades, Calif.: Goodyear, 1972.

Roediger, David R. *The Wages of Whiteness: Race and the Making of the American Working Class*. London and New York: Verso, 1993.

Salzinger, Leslie. *Genders in Production: Making Workers in Mexico's Global Factories*. Berkeley: University of California Press, 2003.

Sennett, Richard, and Jonathan Cobb. *The Hidden Injuries of Class*. New York: W. W. Norton, 1993.

Sheppard, Harold L., and Neal Q. Herrick. *Where Have All the Robots Gone? Worker Dissatisfaction in the '70s*. New York: Free Press, 1972.

Tocqueville, Alexis de. *American Institutions and Their Influence*, with notes by John C. Spencer. New York: A. S. Barnes, 1855.

——. *Democracy in America, and Two Essays on America*, trans. Gerald E. Bevan, intro. Isaac Kramnick. London: Penguin, 2003.

Weber, Max. *From Max Weber: Essays in Sociology*, trans. and ed. Hans Heinrich Gerth, and C. Wright Mills. New York: Oxford University Press, 1969.

——. *Economy and Society: An Outline of Interpretive Sociology*, ed. Guenther Roth and Claus Wittich. Berkeley: University of California Press, 1978.

——. *The Protestant Ethic and the Spirit of Capitalism*. Los Angeles: Roxbury, 2000.

West, Cornel. *Race Matters*. Boston: Beacon Press, 1993.

White, Harrison C. *Markets from Networks: Socioeconomic Models of Production*. Princeton, NJ: Princeton University Press, 2002.

5 Concluding Thoughts

Alford, Robert R. *The Craft of Inquiry: Theories, Methods, Evidence*. New York: Oxford University Press, 1998.

Aronowitz, Stanley. *How Class Works: Power and Social Movement*. New Haven and London: Yale University Press, 2003.

Aronowitz, Stanley, and William DiFazio. *The Jobless Future: Sci-Tech and the Dogma of Work*. Minneapolis: University of Minnesota Press, 1994.

Bourgois, Philippe I. *In Search of Respect: Selling Crack in El Barrio*. Cambridge and New York: Cambridge University Press, 1996.

Butler, Judith. *Gender Trouble: Feminism and the Subversion of Identity*. New York: Routledge, 1990.

Chancer, Lynn S. *Sadomasochism in Everyday Life: The Dynamics of Power and Powerlessness*. New Brunswick, NJ: Rutgers University Press, 1992.

——. *Reconcilable Differences: Confronting Beauty, Pornography, and the Future of Feminism*. Berkeley: University of California Press, 1998.

——. *High-Profile Crimes: When Legal Cases Become Social Causes.* Chicago: University of Chicago Press, 2005.

Connell, R. W. *Masculinities.* Berkeley: University of California Press, 1995.

Ehrenreich, Barbara. *Nickel and Dimed: On (Not) Getting By in America.* New York: Metropolitan Books, 2001.

Fromm, Erich. *Escape from Freedom.* New York: Henry Holt, 1994.

Massey, Douglas S., and Nancy A. Denton. *American Apartheid: Segregation and the Making of the Underclass.* Cambridge, Mass.: Harvard University Press, 1993.

Rollins, Judith. *Between Women: Domestics and Their Employers.* Labor and Social Change. Philadelphia: Temple University Press, 1985.

Schwartz, Joseph. *The Future of Democratic Equality: Rebuilding Social Solidarity in a Fragmented America* (New York: Routledge, forthcoming March 2006).

Index